work hard.
play hard.

work hard.
play hard.

WHY EVERY PASTOR NEEDS A SABBATICAL

GUY MELTON

Work Hard. Play Hard. Copyright © 2025 by Guy Melton. All rights reserved. No portion of this book may be reproduced, stored in a retrieval system, distributed, or transmitted in any form or by any means, except for brief quotations in printed reviews, without prior permission of author. Requests may be submitted by email: info@visitoasis.org

ISBN: 978-0-9883311-9-8 *paperback*
978-0-9883311-8-1 *eBook*

Unless otherwise noted, Scripture is taken from the Holy Bible, New International Version®, NIV® Copyright © 1973, 1978, 1984, 2011 by Biblica, Inc.® Used by permission. All rights reserved worldwide.

Scripture quotations marked KJV are taken from the King James Version. Public domain.

Scripture quotations marked MSG are taken from THE MESSAGE. Copyright © 1993, 2002, 2018 by Eugene H. Peterson. Used by permission of NavPress. All rights reserved. Represented by Tyndale House Publishers, a Division of Tyndale House Ministries.

Formatting by ChristianEditingandDesign.com

Dedication

I dedicate this book to the many council members who have served on our church council over the years. There are too many men and women to name; however, you know who you are. Our church is blessed each year to have such dedicated Christ-followers who, within your roles, serve our church, our pastors, and our staff. I dedicate these pages to those who said yes to be in the council—from the very first council back in the fall of 1991, our nine men and women who started the church with Tonia and me with our first annual budget of $65,000 and no staff, to the council who recently approved (and now oversees our budget) the largest budget in our history of $4 million. Our council's faith, wisdom, and generosity over the years have made Oasis Church the special place it is.

Years ago, our church council realized their pastors needed a sabbatical. They graciously and unanimously voted to bless our pastors and help ensure their health for the present and future ministry. Oasis is a much stronger church because of *you*. I honor you and pray for God's continued richest blessings on you and your families.

Contents

Dedication	5
Acknowledgments	9
Introduction	11
1. Work Hard. Play Hard.	15
2. The Biblical Basis of a Sabbatical	23
3. Why the Resistance to Sabbaticals?	33
4. Why Every Pastor Needs a Sabbatical	53
5. Isn't Vacation Enough? What's the Difference?	79
6. I Would Rather Burn Out Than Rust Out	87
7. Give Him a Sabbatical or Lose Him	95
8. Planning the Church Sabbatical Policy	105
9. Planning the Sabbatical	115
Final Thoughts	119
Conclusion	135
Appendix	139
Additional Resources	153
Works Cited	157
Endnotes	161

Acknowledgments

There is no way to acknowledge all those who were so instrumental in this book and the establishment of sabbaticals for our Oasis pastors without beginning with my wife, Tonia. In our fifty years of marriage and ministry, she has taken on many tasks and dealt with some of the seemingly crazy decisions I've made in ministry. Her calling into ministry proceeded with mine, and I don't think I could have made it this far without her. Tonia is a person of great faith, prayer, generosity, and ministry to others. I could write a book about her faith and ministry alone.

Babe, thanks for standing by me in every decision and calling. You are amazing. Thanks for holding down the house and many other things while I've enjoyed numerous sabbaticals. Thanks for making so many sacrifices for which I could never repay you. (I have forgiven you for firing me from mowing the lawn and cleaning the pool while I was on my first sabbatical, but I'm glad I still don't have to do them.) I love you—happy *fiftieth* anniversary.

I am especially grateful to one of our church council chairmen, Dennis DaCosta. When the council first considered the sabbatical policy, Dennis, a former pastor himself who understood the stress and pressure pastors constantly face, championed the policy for our council and church. His support and leadership were what made it happen. Sabbaticals were a totally foreign thought in our type of church at the time, and—if not for Dennis—it would have been a much tougher journey. Thanks, Dennis, for your lifelong friendship and for blessing me and now so many other pastors and churches with this gift of the sabbatical.

Introduction

Do you need another book on leadership, another "how-to" on church growth, or another guide on x, y, and z? Maybe you do, and that is great—no problem!

Since the world came to a standstill with the start of the COVID-19 pandemic in the spring of 2020, the themes on leadership growth and guides exploded unexpectedly. I now hear fewer pastors wanting more conferences or how-to books, since the unprecedented question we all faced: How to grow a church in a post-pandemic world? No one could claim expertise in this area of ministry.

Even now, if someone claims to have expertise or wants you to read their latest book or attend their latest seminar on post-pandemic church growth, I would run from them. At the least, I'd look at them and what they are offering with a skeptical eye.

I have heard several versions of the following statements and questions: The pandemic knocked the wind out of me and took away any momentum I (or my church) had. What will ministry be like in the years to come? What will happen next? How will the next generation react to the new realities that have challenged the globe, from the multinational corporations to the mom-and-pop spots down the street (if they even endured)? I also heard others say they aren't sure they can handle ministry for the long haul, and some have questioned whether the church will even survive.

Pastors are quitting the ministry in far greater numbers than I have ever seen. There is more talk of burnout, mental illness, heartbrokenness, and discouragement among pastors and church leaders than I have ever experienced.

These questions are not new. They've been with us since before the appearance of the early church, although in today's unique context, they are being exhibited in a slightly different way. Maybe the terms and the culture are not the same, but the realities of burnout, stress, and discouragement in ministry have not been recently discovered.

Just look at the story of Elijah and the depression he went through to the point of asking God to finish his life. I mean, that was some significant discouragement. If one of the greatest men of God in the entire Bible had to deal with these feelings, then why wouldn't you and I be found struggling and grinding away in our little neck of the woods, most of the time in obscurity?

If you are fortunate not to be doing ministry alone and have other staff and lay leaders holding up your arms as Aaron and Hur did with Moses (Exodus 17:11–13), good for you, but you will still face the same feelings at some point, whether you're surrounded by a team or an entire church of supportive people.

Yes, Moses had some incredible guys who held his arms up in battle, but eventually, they had to leave. They had families and lives of their own. So, what did he do then? The same as you and me: he wrestled with discouragement, hurt, and physical fatigue, to name a few challenges.

Yes, post-pandemic ministry is distinct from anything I have faced or dealt with in my almost fifty years in full-time ministry. But ministry has always been difficult. Today, we face the uncertainties of the future and the bleak predictions not only within the church but also from the outside media and culture, which seem to be almost celebrating the demise of the church in America and Christianity as a whole.

I don't need to comment on the culture wars or the political battles within and outside the church. The many winds that are buffeting the church and pastors are too numerous to even mention on these pages, and frankly, I don't think I need to. The last few paragraphs might have caused you to stop and put this book down. It sounds too bleak and pessimistic. You don't need another missal about what is wrong with your church and how hard things are. So, before you stop reading and throw this aside, let us stop. I promise it will get better.

I have some great news and a few answers on maneuvering the rough seas of this twenty-first century. They are not secrets, and most importantly, they are not new. They are not just "quite old" but ancient.

God has given us a road map on how to not only survive but thrive amid the challenges we face. He will help us overcome even if He does not remove all the obstacles. I promise to uncover God's great examples to His children, which, to my dismay, you mostly see it used successfully in the business world, academia, and the medical profession.

This book focuses on you, your church, and how you can institute a sabbatical ministry. It aims to help you have a long-term, healthy ministry, family, and marriage (if you are married). Yes, you need a sabbatical. And yes, your church needs a sabbatical from you. If you and your church do not begin to take one, I predict one or both of you will not only suffer but also stand the chance of crashing and burning in any number of ways.

Taking sabbaticals can be the key to unlocking some of the most impactful personal and ministry successes you have ever had. Most pastors and churches never experience the great benefits of rest and renewal (that famous "R&R"); however, I must warn and clarify: A sabbatical is *not* a vacation.

1

Work Hard. Play Hard.

"Work hard, play hard" has been a motto of mine for many years—I am not sure where I got it, but it stuck. I can go back as far as being a five-year-old and remember how my father would bring me along to open his little neighborhood store at 5:00 a.m. in Temple Terrace, a suburb of Tampa, Florida. I have been working in some form or another ever since—and I must say—I have loved work. My father also loved it, and his work ethic and entrepreneurship are his legacy to me. He never had to drag, beg, or entice me to get me to come to work (although that little donut-making machine was fun to operate, and even better was eating those donuts straight out of the oil).

From those days after our family moved to South Florida, my father, who sadly was an alcoholic and yet still a hard worker, would go to work with a Budweiser in his hand, come home after a long day with a Busch beer, and drink many others in between; I do not know how he could drink so much that he would stumble up the sidewalk late at night after spending hours in the local bar but still get up the following day and go to work at 5:00 a.m. He worked hard and played hard; I got it from him, I guess (minus the alcohol, of course). To this day, I will not touch a drop of alcohol because of what it did to our family. It not only destroyed our wonderful home but also my father's life; however, with his genes, I believe I inherited the work addiction.

During my elementary years, every day after school, I would jump on my bike and ride over to the Little General store (the 7-11s of the day) and help the guy at the counter. I would sweep, stack the soda bottles, load the coolers, and do anything else he wanted me to do. The owner would give me about $1.00 a day, but mind you, Coke was only 10¢ back then, and I could play a lot of pinball games with that. Predictably, I got addicted to pinball. Addiction runs deep in our family. Generations deep. There were no digital games back then; you just loaded a dime or a quarter into the machine and started hitting the ball from one side to the other. Playing pinball was a rush, and I still remember it today. When I got old enough to have a neighborhood paper route (back then, they used to deliver something called a "newspaper" to the front of people's homes), I graduated from a few dollars a week to about $10 a week and a lot of Saturday afternoon pinball games after collecting the 25¢ from the customers each week. Sometimes, I would even spend all my earnings on pinball on just one Saturday afternoon.

Do you see a pattern here? A "work hard, play hard" motto *and* an addictive personality. Since I became a Christian at six years old, my godly mom took us to church, even after her divorce. Though she worked two jobs seven days a week, we still attended church and Sunday school. Mom even taught Sunday school in the morning, went to work, and came after work for Sunday night service. No, she was *not* a workaholic. She hated work but knew how to work and support her four children. Mom gave us all the basics, for which I will be forever grateful. She loved the Lord, and I am thankful for the legacy she left behind for me and my siblings. Because of her own faith, my Christian life grew, and at twelve years of age, I became convicted that all the money I made I was throwing down the pinball machine. I was addicted to work and play, so I quit. To this day, I doubt I have played five pinball games since then, although simply seeing a pinball machine still provokes a rush in me.

Church planting years

Fast-forward many years to 1991. After serving at my home church for thirteen years straight out of college, God called me west of our city in Broward County to the new and growing City of Pembroke Pines. With a small core group of nine other adults, Tonia and I, and our three young sons, we began what is now known—more than thirty years later—as the Oasis Church of South Florida.

I have been known for saying that I could never start a church (or do what we now call church planting). Church planting is as scary and hard nowadays as it was back then. I did not have all it took then or now; however, God said to do it, and by His grace, we did it.

I took the challenge and the call from God and jumped in with everything I had, seven days a week. When you start a business or a church, it takes everything you have to survive. And this was true for us then: with a growing family and a new home we had bought just before God called us to leave a pastoral staff position at my home church (and a sizable cut in salary). So, we worked hard, but there was not much time to play hard; we were in a "sink or swim" mode. Some of you reading this right now identify with me—you know what a rat race pastoral ministry can be. Well, ramp that up 100 percent if you are planting a church but with far fewer resources.

Despite our hard work, fear of the unknown, and all the *if-we-could-do-these* moments, God was and has been faithful for over three decades and counting. Our little city began to grow. Hurricane Andrew—still one of the most devastating hurricanes in American history—hit in 1992, just a year after we started our church in a humble little trailer in the middle of what was Everglades mud. South Florida has been built on the black, yucky mud (called "muck" down here) of the Everglades. While Pembroke Pines saw hurricane-strength winds and sustained minor damage, it was nothing like southern Dade County south of Miami, where thousands became homeless and lost everything.

There was no need to stay in the South Dade County area because not much was left; entire towns had been wiped out. What did these families do? They moved north, and the City of Pembroke Pines went from a city of 60,000 to over 185,000 in a short time. For three straight years, we were among the top three fastest-growing cities in the United States.

Being in proximity to Miami, God continued sending people from South Dade and around the world. Our core group of eleven church members grew to hundreds. One service in a trailer became five services, and we were building a new building. With all the excitement of the growth and what God was doing, I lost my voice—not for a day, but every Sunday. After five services, my voice would be shot. I would do everything I could to nurse it back to health for the following Sunday and start all over. My voice issues continued to worsen, and all the while, I was overseeing a new building project, five services, a growing church, and adding staff.

Do not think for a moment I was not enjoying it—I loved it. I thrive on work, remember? I thrive on stress. I believe I am a carrier of it. But during this season of life with teenagers, moving into middle age, and working seven days a week, my body began to say, "Hold it, big boy. You can't keep doing this."

Unexpected happenings

It began with months of doctor's visits to discover what was happening to my voice. The final diagnosis was nodules on the vocal cords. I had a choice of having either surgery or months of therapy and no speaking, meetings, or counseling. No more standing at the door to greet hundreds of our church members—also, no preaching and no standing at the doorway to say goodbye at the end of service. My ministry came to a grinding halt that day when the doctor said, "You must either change your lifestyle or career." What was my response? "Doctor,

I have no choice: I don't have a career—I have a calling. I must do what it takes."

I will not go into all it took but let me say this: my whole life changed, from the diet I had (or did not have) to my meetings and my entire schedule. On that day, I immediately penned a letter to our church family to inform them what was happening and that, starting the following week, our youth pastor and worship pastor would begin to preach with me. Shortly after, we added another pastor to our team, which marked the beginning of our "teaching team" at Oasis Church. To this day, I preach at most twice a month. After the pandemic, we are now only offering three services, but it takes all I can do to do them. Our church adapted, and so have I. At one time, we had as many as seven men and women on our teaching team. At one point, we even had as many as fourteen services a week on three campuses. Yet, since I received my diagnosis, I've only preached one or two Sundays a month.

With this massive change in my health, life, and ministry, I still did not consider a sabbatical. Every summer, I would take July off from the pulpit to rest my voice but continued working through it. I am not sure if I even fully comprehended what a pastoral sabbatical was at the time. I had probably only heard of it for educators but not for preachers.

After fourteen incredible years of pastoring Oasis Church and seeing remarkable growth, new buildings, and hundreds of new people join our congregation, Hurricane Wilma hit Pembroke Pines in October 2005. Unlike Hurricane Andrew, Wilma inflicted considerable damage on our then five-year-old building, including having a quarter of the roof torn off, which led to two years' worth of repairs, insurance, and delays. As we were reeling from this and trying to figure out how to meet in a building with a broken roof, I lost the three full-time staff who had been with me for the entire first fourteen years. Initially, they had come in as volunteers, then transitioned to part-time staff, and eventually became permanent church planters alongside me. However, within one month, they were all gone. The new personnel around me, including our youth pastor, tried to regroup; we had no choice but to do so. However, the loss of these good friends shook me.

I had not lost a single staff member in the fourteen years since we started the church, but suddenly, my three senior members were all gone. Without digging deeper, I had been unaware of some issues in their lives and marriages; despite this, our congregation questioned my leadership and what I must have done to cause it.

I am not prone to depression or discouragement. I push through. I will make it happen one way or the other. I thrive on stress, right? But something told me I had better get a grip on this if I were to make it through the long haul. I suspected there was something just not right. I could not keep this pace forever.

The following months brought us to this book you are reading now. After much hard work, meetings, readings, and searching out the ins and outs of sabbaticals, we formulated a plan to present to our church council and, ultimately, to our church family. This led to the official launch of Oasis sabbaticals, and I am deeply grateful that God led our church to implement a sabbatical policy. I would not be the pastor of Oasis Church (and possibly be out of the ministry altogether) today if God did not lead our church to establish this God-blessed and ordained practice.

Now, it's time to write your story.

In the following chapters, I hope that you and your church will find encouragement to adopt or enhance your pastoral sabbatical policy. In the following pages, I will give my all to help you and your leadership envision how you can implement the sabbatical policy. You may even find that you must put this policy into action if you and your church want to move beyond surviving to thriving.

What about *work hard, play hard*, you ask?

It's still my motto!

2

The Biblical Basis of a Sabbatical

I've wrestled with this chapter more than any other in the book because I did not think you needed it. I did not want to do it. I *decided* not to do it. Anyone reading this book will likely be familiar with the meaning of the Sabbath and its connection to taking a sabbatical, right? Of course! So, after a needless and ridiculous amount of time and energy, which included prayer, I have decided to write this chapter, not because I think you do not understand the biblical Sabbath. Many of you may even know more than I do.

What I am *not* going to do is make an exhaustive study, as I have sometimes read when scholars discuss the Sabbath in the Old Testament versus the New Testament and today. I will not start discussing why many Christians nowadays worship on the first day of the week. There are already plenty of articles and even books written about the subject. I don't need to teach theology or discuss the differences that various religious groups and even individual Christians might have on choosing one day of the week as the Lord's own, or all that surrounds how to celebrate or practice it. What I would like to do instead is draw a straight line from the Sabbath in the Old and New Testaments and discuss why it is so deeply rooted in today's concept of pastoral sabbaticals.

Yes, in many cases, the secular world does sabbaticals better than the church does. Professionals in the medical field[1], education[2], and now multinational companies[3] have found the value of sabbaticals. As in finances, when anyone (even someone who does not acknowledge God) utilizes His biblical financial principles, God's proposition is honored and works even if we're not blessed with Christ's new life. God is into the simple and practical. He doesn't try to hide things from us. As a result of their sabbatical policies, many secular (I would even go as far as calling some of them "godless" and even "anti-God") businesses can thrive. They are practicing biblical principles and may not even know it—handling money in God's way, by investing it and giving it, will work for anyone who applies it, and the same pertains to the practice of taking sabbaticals. From the time of the Bible, God gave straightforward instructions to rest.

Even though God did not need to rest after creating the world in six days, what did He do? He rested. It was a model for us who needed to learn this life's best rhythms, and it showed us how valuable this concept is, that even the Creator of all things, *rested* (Genesis 2:1–3).

If we are created in His image, we should follow His lead. This is not hard to understand: He stepped back to admire His handiwork of those past six days. As such, He calls on *us* to take a step back, reflect on the hard work we've accomplished, and *rest*.

God felt that resting was so essential for His creation that He enshrined it in the Ten Commandments. Now, I know we do not always live by the Ten Commandments, but none of us questions their wisdom, righteousness, and the wisdom of following them.

Without saying more about the Ten Commandments, let me share His reminder of this significant directive:

> Remember the Sabbath day by keeping it holy. Six days you shall labor and do all your work, but the seventh day is a sabbath to the Lord your God. On it you shall not do any work, neither you, nor your son or daughter, nor your male or female servant, nor your animals, nor any foreigner residing in your towns. For in six days, the Lord made the heavens and the earth, the sea, and all that is in them, but he rested on the seventh day. Therefore the Lord blessed the Sabbath day and made it holy. (Exodus 20:8–11)

While studying for a message to our church on rest and the Sabbath, I read a book[4] where the author pointed out that this commandment on the Sabbath in Exodus is actually the longest in the Ten Commandments. WOW! How could I have missed this after all these years? While commands against murder, lying, cheating, and adultery are each given just one line in Exodus, the command to observe the Sabbath is a full paragraph. Could it be that—just like us, who reveal what is most important by how we spend our time and what we talk about—God might have highlighted here the importance of rest and worship? That is a powerful thought. Then, a few verses up, you read the second-longest command: "You shall have no other gods before me."

As pastors, we preach this all the time, but simply look at your calendar and checkbook, and it will tell you what you think are the most important things in your life. We preach not to make idols out of hobbies, jobs, relationships, and things, yet, if we ourselves put them ahead of living out our faith and are too busy to take time away to rest, is it possible that our calling and our ministry have become idols to us?

It's hard to look in the mirror, but both commandments are linked together as a message from God in their importance. Yes, this is the English Bible translation; however, we can't separate the length that God went to in giving these commandments to us.

Before you dismiss this as something you've already heard about taking time off, let me reassure you: I am working toward something that has entirely revolutionized my thinking on sabbaticals. I was already convinced that sabbaticals are biblical and crucial to a long-term pastorate; however, the Bible never explicitly tells us to take a long, extended rest beyond the day of the Sabbath—which is why I am writing this book. I believe the principle of needful rest as a form of reverence is directly tied to the idea of taking extended time away, and we, as pastors, have missed it, even though it is right before our eyes. After God illuminated my vision of this exciting ancient principle hidden right before my eyes, I am now more excited to encourage other pastors to take sabbaticals.

While God continued to remind His people to rest after slavery in Egypt (Deuteronomy 5:12–15), there is so much more to the Sabbath than that. Yes, we were slaves to sin. Many times, we remain slaves to our calling and ministry. As pastors, we get so caught up in the mission, goals, and numbers that we lose sight of our humanity and the joy of having Jesus Christ as our own sabbath rest. Consider that for a second. Pause and ponder how beautiful it is that our Lord is the *Lord of the Sabbath*: "Then he said to them, 'The Sabbath was made for man, not man for the Sabbath. So the Son of Man is Lord even of the Sabbath'" (Mark 2:27–28).

Growing up, I was taught (more by action than words) to "Work hard, don't worry about resting or days off; you have eternity to rest." True in life, perhaps, but *not* biblically true. I do look forward to eternity, and the older I get, the more I look forward to that day to spend eternity with my Lord. But I don't necessarily want to enter eternity because I worked myself to death, which is the direct opposite of offering my body as the temple of the Holy Spirit.

There is a beautiful passage in Hebrews chapter 4 that speaks of our eternal rest and gives us these wonderful words to hold on to:

> For if Joshua had given them rest, God would not have spoken later about another day. There remains, then, a Sabbath-rest for the people of God; for anyone who enters God's rest also rests from their works, just as God did from his. Let us, therefore, make every effort to enter that rest, so that no one will

> perish by following their example of disobedience. (Hebrews 4:8–11)

This remarkable passage, which gives us so much hope, does not have to be limited to hope for the future. God wants us to experience rest and the abundant life He speaks of in John 10: "The thief comes only to steal and kill and destroy; I have come that they may have life, and have it to the full" (John 10:10). We preach and teach others about it, yet we don't practice it ourselves.

You may ask, "But what about that new revelation on sabbaticals you found?" I haven't forgotten about it. Read on.

> The Lord said to Moses at Mount Sinai, "Speak to the Israelites and say to them: 'When you enter the land I am going to give you, the land itself must observe a sabbath to the Lord. For six years sow your fields, and for six years prune your vineyards and gather their crops. But in the seventh year the land is to have a year of sabbath rest, a sabbath to the Lord. Do not sow your fields or prune your vineyards. Do not reap what grows of itself or harvest the grapes of your untended vines. The land is to have a year of rest. Whatever the land yields during the sabbath year will be food for you—for yourself, your male and female servants, and the hired worker and temporary resident who live among you, as well as for your livestock and the wild animals in your land. Whatever the land produces may be eaten. (Leviticus 25:1–7)

Ok, I know you knew I would get to this passage. Before you begin to throw red flags about me taking it out of context, please hear me out: I think this might be the most revolutionary thought and example of the sabbatical in the twenty-first century.

We don't need another teaching on the agricultural culture of the day. I will assume we all understand the principle of giving the crops a rest and the sabbath year of resting the land. God made it clear to His people. There was no mistaking what He wanted and expected. This was before fertilizers and the various methods to replenish the land and soil with the nutrients and balances that plants need for future crops. This works for land, but I'm not sure we've discovered a breakthrough for resting the body, mind, and spirit. If it is out there, I have missed it. I have read multiple articles where our bodies still need a certain amount of rest to replenish us for the next day. Just as God supplied manna to His people in the Old Testament, He replenishes us daily with the manna of rest we need.

Whether rest is needed by the day, week, vacation, or extended leave, the meaning and necessity remain. Pastors are not superhumans or machines. God's principles apply to us as well—in case we need reminding.

Let us go back to the ground, the land that God wanted to keep replenished and healthy so that the people of God could have food and sustenance. This ancient passage, which is easy to discount, presents the strongest argument for an extended time away. God said to leave the land alone, not to work it or do anything for a year. Yes, He wanted to replenish the land. But what was happening to His people during that time? They were resting. The Lord didn't say go out and get more land or go out and get another job to feed your family. No, the Scripture implied that they also did not work. Is this a stretch? I don't think so. Can you find anywhere that He gave them alternative plans? It is common sense that you will cease working if you have lost your job. Knowing the need for food would not go away, God allowed a small part of the land to be active just for their families to eat, which makes sense.

Compare making a family garden with having acres and acres of land to till and cultivate by hand, water by hand, and utilizing livestock to help. Everyone gets a rest, even the animals. Are you seeing it? This natural period of human rest was a by-product of the sabbath of the land. We mark our lives by seasons. The farmer plans their work by the seasons. The Bible tells us there is a season for planting, watering, and reaping the harvest. The writer of Ecclesiastes reminds us that there is a season for all things.

As a new year descends on us each January, one of the first things we do is start planning for the various seasons of the coming year. The form this planning takes may be a church or personal calendar filled with vacations, trips, or personal events, marking the seasons that shape our lives.

Farmers understood the seasons and lived by them, which meant there was a season for rest from work. God ordained rest, but He also ordained the sabbatical season—whether you want to call it that or not—He gave the land and the landowner a year off for rest and restoration.

I am not suggesting you start with a yearlong sabbatical that could end your ministry where you are or put you into a spiral of fear and boredom if you have never taken more than a couple of weeks off. (I doubt many of us have taken even two weeks back-to-back; if so, it's been rare.)

Fast-forward thousands of years. You and I need a sabbath. Not just a day every week, but at least once every seventh year. How do we survive? Just as the children of God had an avenue provided through their family garden, which even the children could tend to, we must have a way to survive, whether for a month, three months, six months, or sometimes even up to a year.

That is what the church is for. As other farmers provide food and crops for the farmer on sabbatical with their land, the church provides for the pastor (farmer) during his sabbatical. If the church is to provide for pastors and the shepherds who give their lives and are worthy of double honor, then it's a no-brainer that the church should provide during a sabbatical.

This discussion naturally leads to the how-to chapters of sabbaticals, and we will discuss that subject in more detail then. Just so you know where I am headed, I believe *every* pastor, whether you are in the smallest of churches or not, can take a sabbatical, and the church can help provide for them. In the following chapters, I will outline the steps to make it happen. Not all churches can offer full salaries and benefits, but there are other options out there you may not have considered. Whether you see what I see in Leviticus or not, we all know God wants us to rest and take sabbath rest.

Let the land and farmers rest! You and your church will be the better for it.

3

Why the Resistance to Sabbaticals?

One of the biggest obstacles and enemies to your long-term church ministry and your private life is the resistance most pastors and churches face when people hear the term '*sabbatical.*' I have heard it all. I can't imagine you can give me a reason not to take a sabbatical that I have not heard yet. Many are legit, and some are simply a smoke screen for other fears and motives. This resistance is normal. And truth be told, there are some incredibly good concerns and hindrances to instituting the biblical sabbatical.

In the following pages, we will tackle some of the more prominent concerns in more detail because if you are paralyzed by *why* you can't take a sabbatical, then you never will, and you will miss God's greatest ministry in store for you.

So, let's get to it!

While I'm not sure there is a #1 reason, there are certainly some that I've struggled with, and most everyone I've ever talked to about sabbaticals struggles with the same issues. This is not a comprehensive list, and most of these will be discussed in more detail as we move through the book together.

1. **Why should I, as a pastor, get an extended time away when most of my congregation do not get a sabbatical leave?**

True, most church staff and members do not get a sabbatical in your congregation. It does not vary much from the CEO of a large corporation to the retail clerk at your neighborhood retail store, and everything in between. Some statistics show that between 4 and 17 percent of businesses in the past have offered a sabbatical or, as some refer to it, "extended leave." However, this trend is growing, and the COVID-19 pandemic has accelerated the practice of taking longer time away. I believe it will increase greatly in the future.

Pastors have a unique role compared to most other careers or roles. Let me begin by highlighting that pastoring is a calling and *a calling from God* at that. It is not just a voluntary role that the pastor chose to undertake. (Some might, but normally, they do not last in ministry.)

Ministry for a pastor is 24 hours a day, 365 days a year—even on a day off. A pastor may receive calls to a hospital, a funeral, a family crisis, and numerous other situations. This has happened to every pastor many times over our ministry years. It does not matter if you are on vacation. I am known to have said that I am never on vacation because any crisis at church is my responsibility to address or respond to. It has already happened several times while writing this book, during the study and writing month that our church council has given me. This time away is a gift, but it does not mean I am away other than geographically.

Pastors do not just study for a sermon. They do not go in at 9:00 a.m. and go home at 5:00 p.m. We are available to shepherd our congregants during late nights and sometimes even spend all night in the hospital at the bedside of a dying church member. All this takes a toll; yes, we know. However, it is worth highlighting that this toll compounds over the years. Pastors also provide pastoral counseling (with some even becoming licensed counselors) to those experiencing the loss of a job or a loved one, the death of a marriage, and struggle through these challenges with them.

I don't even know how to put into words the stress, the emotional drain, and the physical toll it takes if you are a full-time pastor. I recall once being on a cruise, only to receive a call stating that two of my church council members had resigned, not just from the council, but also from the church. They were godly people who had been active in our church for years, but because of one decision I had to make regarding their favorite staff person, they quit. My cruise was ruined, and ultimately, Tonia had to know, so she had to deal with it as well.

These are staff issues that may happen as a church grows. During a strenuous season, I almost quit taking my yearly week of vacation in the fall, my favorite time of year (except for Christmas week), because it seemed every time I did, I would lose a staff member, or other major issues would arise within the church. And I do not just mean someone went to the hospital or got laid off. Understandably, that is major to them, but that is not what I mean. Pastors are humans. We internalize these things. We do not lay a tool down on Friday, walk away from the job for the weekend, and pick it back up on Monday. We do not turn our phones off on our days off or vacations. We can always be reachable, even more so in this age of instant communication.

Pastors carry the load of a shepherd because God called us to be His shepherds for His children. The Bible says we will be judged to a higher standard because of the honor our role brings. Shepherds do not leave their sheep and go home at night. No, they are always watching over and caring for them. Hebrews 13 tells us that pastors carry a heavy burden, not just as examples to follow; and it also reminds us that God will judge us to a higher level: "Remember your leaders, who spoke the word of God to you. Consider the outcome of their way of life and imitate their faith" (Hebrews 13:7). That is still scary today after almost fifty years of full-time ministry. 1 Peter 5:1-4 is another passage that carries a huge and heavy weight for pastors, as we will stand before God and be judged for how we, as shepherds, loved and cared for our sheep. Who wants that pressure? Most do not, but as I said earlier, this is not a career but a calling. If you are called, you'd better be obedient and respond as Isaiah did in Isaiah 6: "Here am I, Lord. Send me!" (Isaiah 6:8).

Preparing sermons is just one small part of a pastor's role, but it is a huge responsibility that few ever fully understand. You are teaching God's Word, not yours. He is watching. I take it very seriously, and most pastors do as well. We are also being compared with every TV and nationally known pastor, building up the pressure.

The pressure on the pastor grows with each new member, convert, and disciple. Add to that success in numbers (from the world's perspective), increased services bringing hundreds of details and entailing more people to deal with and lead. In his post "Why are Preachers so Exhausted After Preaching?"[5] Pastor M.R. Perry suggests that bringing the message on Sunday is like working an eight-hour day. This is due to the strain, stress, and emotional toll that teaching and bringing the Word of God to His people takes. I cannot fully explain it, but I do feel it. If you then add another service, then three, then four, or, as we have done at Oasis Church in the past, add five services on the weekend and preach them consecutively, it is exhausting. This is why Sunday afternoon is the only day of the week I take naps. I am exhausted in every way, physically, spiritually, emotionally, and mentally. As they say, I am wasted. Then, we head back to leadership meetings or other Sunday meetings.

Now, I am not complaining. I am honored to have been called to pastoring. Like most pastors, I am humbled to do ministry for a living. I know it doesn't sound like it after the last couple of paragraphs, but the question we are answering is why pastors should get a sabbatical compared to everyone else, and I answered. This is in no way to disparage or belittle what others are called to and do for a living. Everything we do, if God has called us or led us to do, is just as important. We are not comparing importance. A pastor is no more important than anyone else as a person. We are speaking of the roles we fill. While other roles and callings can carry extreme weight and stress, and their duties may also call to be above reproach, etc., the role of the pastor teaching the whole counsel of the Gospel of Christ to His church is unique in that it will be judged with greater strictness than anything else (James 3:1). I could go on and on. Still, I can sum this up by saying that a sabbatical for a shepherd is a *gift*. It is a precious gift to any pastor and might be the difference between life and death. If not that dramatic, it might be the gift of longevity in a pastor's ministry.

Here is a little taste of the expectations of pastors, a report from one pastoral search committee as they searched for the perfect pastor:

Pastoral Search Report

> We do not have a happy report to give. We've not been able to find a suitable candidate for this church, though we still have one promising prospect. We do appreciate all the suggestions from the church members, and we've followed up each one with interviews or calling at least three references. The following is our confidential report on the present candidates.
>
> **Adam**: Good man but problems with his wife. Also one reference told of how his wife and he enjoy walking nude in the woods.

Noah: Former pastorate of twelve years with no converts. Prone to unrealistic building projects.

Abraham: Though the references reported wife-swapping, the facts seem to show he never slept with another man's wife, but did offer to share his own wife with another man.

Joseph: A big thinker, but a braggart, believes in dream-interpreting, and has a prison record.

Moses: A modest and meek man, but he's a poor communicator, even stuttering at times. Sometimes blows his stack and acts rashly. Some say he left an earlier church over a murder charge.

David: The most promising leader of all until we discovered the affair he had with his neighbor's wife.

Solomon: Great preacher, but our parsonage would never hold all those wives.

Elijah: Prone to depression—collapses under pressure.

Elisha: Reported to have lived with a single widow while at his former church.

Hosea: A tender and loving pastor, but our people could never handle his wife's occupation.

Deborah: Female.

Jeremiah: Emotionally unstable, alarmist, negative, always lamenting things, and reported to have taken a long trip to bury his underwear on the bank of foreign river.

Isaiah: On the fringe? Claims to have seen angels in church. Has trouble with his language.

Jonah: Refused God's call into ministry until he was forced to obey by getting swallowed up by a great fish. He told us the fish later spit him out on the shore near here. We hung up.

Amos: Too backward and unpolished. With some seminary training he might have promise, but has a hang-up against wealthy people. Might fit in better in a poor congregation.

John: Says he is a Baptist, but definitely doesn't dress like one. Has slept in the outdoors for months on end, has a weird diet, and provokes denominational leaders.

Peter: Too blue collar. Has a bad temper—even has been known to curse. Had a big run-in with Paul in Antioch. Aggressive, but a loose cannon.

Paul: Powerful CEO type leader and fascinating preacher. However, short on tact, unforgiving with younger ministers, harsh and has been known to preach all night.

Timothy: Too young.

Jesus: Has had popular times, but once when his church grew to 5000 he managed to offend them all and this church dwindled down to twelve people. Seldom stays in one place very long. And, of course, he's single.

Judas: His references are solid. A steady plodder. Conservative. Good connections. Knows how to handle money. We're inviting him to preach this Sunday. Possibilities here.[6]

And here's what Oasis Church will want someday when this imperfect pastor is gone—inspired by a survey that compiles qualities that people expect from the perfect pastor.[7]

The Perfect Pastor

- Preaches exactly twelve minutes.
- Frequently condemns sin but never upsets anyone.
- Works from 8:00 a.m. until midnight and is also a janitor.
- Makes $60 a week, wears good clothes, buys good books, drives a good car, and gives about $80 a week to the poor.
- Twenty-eight years of age and have been preaching for thirty years.
- Wonderfully gentle and good-looking.

- A burning desire to work with teenagers, but is always with the senior citizens.

- Makes fifteen daily calls to church families, visits shut-ins and the hospitalized, evangelizes the unchurched, and is always in the office when needed.

DISCLAIMER: This is not an exhaustive list, but rather a starting point.

Well, I think you get my point about why the pastor should be the first to receive the sabbatical leave. Now, let's go to point number two of those major concerns that may prevent you from taking a sabbatical.

2. Our church can't afford our pastor to be gone and pay him.

I argue that you can't afford not to give your pastor a sabbatical unless you are hoping to get a better pastor in a few years. In that case, keep doing what you are doing. Most pastors stay between two and a half and five years in one place—five years is a lot these days. They will get a "sabbatical" one way or another. Usually, there are lapses of time between churches, which serve as sabbatical time for them, even though they do not receive the same benefits or rewards as a true sabbatical.

The church then must spend a lot of money exploring other pastors from different places—which has high costs—not just in time but also in money for the search, the lost momentum in ministry, and the loss of a shepherd for sometimes up to two years.

The church committee must visit other churches, look, bring pastors in, pay others to find candidates, and then do it all over in two to five years. The price of this far outweighs spending some extra money you are saving for the rainy day, the remodel, the next outreach, or the missions project. Yes, I said it out loud. You might need to take some money for another ministry and invest it in *your church's future*. Please highlight the words "your church" in the last sentence, and notice it doesn't say "in his future." True, your church's sabbatical leave for your pastor will benefit him, his ministry, and his family. Still, it will help your church even more in the long run if you have a better, more rested, spiritually healthy pastor.

The cost to the church of constantly turning over pastors is beyond dollars, but it does translate into untold dollars missed or spent because of not finding a way to pay your pastor for a month or three or six. I truly believe almost every church, though not all, can afford to pay their pastor while away and fill the pulpit in his absence. That is the next hesitation and question.

3. If our pastor leaves for an extended period, how will we fill the pulpit?

This is another legitimate concern. It is a challenge, but not one that any church cannot answer. *Any* church? Did I say *any* church?

Start from within. Why can't another church leader fill the pulpit? Oh, they aren't good enough (tongue in cheek, settle down). Of course, they lack confidence if they have not done it before. They may lack theological training. They may not speak perfectly like you or your pastor can. There are many reasons not to have a layperson fill the pulpit in your pastor's absence, but I believe they can all be addressed and worked out.

That's where Ephesians 4 comes in. If churches and pastors truly believed that gifts are all placed in the church for a purpose and that all gifts are to be joined as a part of the body, then this would not be an issue. If pastors believed the Bible about our role to equip the saints, this would not be an issue either.

Finding someone to cover for you will not happen overnight, but you probably already have laypeople teaching in small groups in your church. You have people who speak in public settings. You have schoolteachers. Why not offer classes and practice sessions on researching, writing, and preaching sermons, or consider a mini-seminar on preaching? Your church will love and support those who fill in for you, and I promise they will cheer them on.

I mentioned in the opening that when I lost my voice due to nodules on my vocal cords, I had to stop preaching for a while and set up a teaching team; our church was extraordinarily supportive of our staff. I did not mention that over the next ten years, our church grew, and we started two more campuses, becoming the only church I know of to have services seven nights a week. We called it 7NOW for Seven Nights Of Worship. All in all, we were doing fourteen services, all live, regularly. And during special times, such as Easter, there would be twenty-one services or more.

I never did more than three services, and most of the time, only two. Our staff pastors did some. We also developed a team, mostly comprised of laymen and a couple of women. Our teaching team has consisted of four to seven men and women over the last twenty-five years.

Maybe some pastors out there fear that others preaching in their pulpit may crush their ego, or they may fear what the untrained lay preachers may say, or . . . so many other hesitations. Embracing these fears will prevent you from unleashing your congregation's gifted people and from taking a sabbatical. This one thing alone will fill your pulpit, regardless of your size. Some might say, "But people will stop coming . . ." and yes, some might. You prepare them, teach them, and explain the biblical and practical truth of having various teachers.

If you think, "How can our church ever grow if I'm not the only speaker?" Well, I had no choice when I got vocal damage and had some of the same concerns. For the record, during the first few years, our church had approximately 500 to 600 members and grew to over 2,400 before the pandemic, which was also before the online church campus expanded during COVID-19. I can make the case that having a plurality of teachers is more biblical than having one celebrity pastor who, when not in the pulpit, is like the Holy Spirit has left the room. This is not true and is more of a cultural issue. It is time to put that to rest, if you will get some rest. We are not talking about being lazy but being smart! You've heard the expression "working smarter, not harder"? This is what it takes to institute the sabbatical policy in your church.

Now, lay teachers and speakers might not be the only avenue. If you have a multi-staff church, then prepare them to have your staff speak for a season.

For years now, every July, our church has had guest speakers come in to teach. We have partnerships with our former staff members, missionaries we support, or longtime supporters of our ministry. Yes, inviting guest speakers has some costs and might not be your answer, but it gives our team of teachers a rest, and our people love getting a rest from hearing us. They might not say it out loud, but they also think about it with you. We even budget it each year. Doing it in this manner is a ministry, too. Missionaries, as well as some of our U.S. inner-city pastors (supported through one of our outreach ministries, called Love Cities, Love Pastors), occasionally come to teach. You are exposing them to your people, and you are exposing your congregants to their ministry. Instead of taking in special speakers during the year, save money on honoraria and be more strategic when you are on sabbatical.

Some churches are part of denominations or groups of churches that have staff members who can come in and speak, or they may have retired pastors and missionaries whom they can call upon. These groups help when a church loses a pastor (more times than not, because they don't get a sabbatical, even though they don't always realize it either).

Most of us have local or not-so-local friends in the ministry who might be willing to fill our pulpit for us. In recent years, we've asked church planters in our local area whom we have supported. They love to speak to a whole different church outside their plant environment, and we get to love and encourage them. Since we have a staff team, our church has also supplied pulpits before. We're limited, but we do. I hope in the years ahead, a big part of my ministry, as I slow down—and the day comes when I won't be able to carry the load of Oasis Church as lead pastor—will be to fill pulpits for guys who need a rest. I hope our Love Cities, Love Pastors ministry can develop this great community resource as well. I know planning and coordinating who is to cover for you may seem like a significant barrier, but it is not a barrier that cannot be worked out in *all* cases. Well, maybe only 99 percent of the time. I know there are sometimes exceptions.

Preparation and planning are probably the most essential keys to making this idea of a pastor's sabbatical happen. In later chapters, we will discuss in greater detail how to prepare the pastor and church for sabbaticals.

4. **If I take a sabbatical, they might fire me while I am away.**

Of course, with churches, anything is possible. It is hard to surprise me anymore, but it can happen, though I have never heard of it happening. I doubt a church that loves its pastor enough to send them on a sabbatical would then replace them. If they do, maybe they don't deserve you, and you are better off. Risks are part of every decision. This should be a low risk. And, of course, you must go with your own gut feeling about the community, the congregation, and the politics/business side of your commitment, as those influence your sense of your own calling as well as your obligations to your family.

5. **If we give our pastor a sabbatical, he may go away and come back to tell us he's leaving.**

Again, this is possible, but unlikely. One way to ensure that this will not happen either with the senior leader or other staff who might get a sabbatical is to institute an agreement as part of your sabbatical policy. In this agreement, the pastor will sign, stating that if they leave within a certain period after their sabbatical, they must reimburse the church for the pay they received while away. Our church makes it a year, but it is up to the church. The love and affirmation you show the pastor should strengthen your bond and his loyalty to your church—you see this happening more often than not.

6. **But how will our church survive without the pastor—he fills so many roles?**

Again, if you are a New Testament church (most reading this book would fall into that category) and you believe the church—as the body of Christ on earth—is made up of many members and that all the members are ministers and are to use their gifts, then why would you worry?

I must admit my greatest fear when I drove out of the parking lot on my first sabbatical in May 2005 was to think of all the unknowns. I was scared to death. By then, I had only been gone more than two weeks at a time once, and that was my cross-country trip with the kids and Tonia. I realized I had not left this baby I'd helped birth, for fifteen years, this church I'd helped plant. It was scary. It was not easy.

I had to keep reminding myself: this is not my church. It is His church. Initially, many in my home church always referred to Oasis Church as "Guy's church." Nope, it'd better not be. If it is *your* church, this is the first thing you must fix today before deciding on a sabbatical. I truly believe most pastors fear this more than anything else. They think they are so important that God's church can't survive without them. We will not say it, but it is true in many cases.

Maybe you should take a sabbatical and put Jesus and His people to the test. They might just survive without you. You think? Let's face it: someday, you will die, retire, or move on. What will they do then? Sabbaticals are a great test to see how well you and the church leadership have done in the Ephesians 4 and 1 Corinthians 12 areas. It doesn't have to be perfect. Yes, there will be hiccups. Jesus had a few hiccups with His twelve, and He is God. How do you think He felt when He left for a sabbatical and left a bunch of misfits to carry out the most important mission ever to: "Go and make disciples and to build *My* church"? If *His* plans have worked for 2,000 years, they would work during your sabbatical. If the church is built on you, maybe it is time to change pastors anyway. I know this is brutally honest, but it is true.

A side note: After four sabbaticals, our church has survived and grown during several of them, and the offerings were not affected. That can be very humbling. Ha!

During my last two prolonged six-month sabbaticals, many people who did not hear me preach and didn't meet me for all those months joined our church. I love this because it shows that the success of Oasis Church is not about me, and they will not be tied to me, but hopefully to Jesus as the head and cornerstone of His church.

7. But who will fill my shoes? I do more than preach.

Refer to previous answers. It is your role as pastor to teach them to minister, not to do the work of the ministry for them.

I have heard it said that if you, as a pastor, want to work yourself to death and be the hero, your church will let you. When you burn out and melt down or die, they will all gather as they did in the South (and might still do), have fried chicken in the fellowship hall, reminisce, and begin to talk about who their next pastor will be. See, you are going to be gone anyway, so start planning and let the church see some benefits from being gone, *before* you go. Prepare them to do the work of the ministry so you can take a sabbatical. If you cannot leave because of how valuable you are, then you aren't doing your job; it's time to start doing what God has called you to do: shepherd and equip the sheep. There are plenty of members in your church who can fill various roles. It might take three, four, or even a dozen since many are laypeople with full-time jobs, but they are there. I learned from building a youth ministry many years ago that you must equip others to grow above the 100-mark in ministry. Most of us can only handle about 100; if you are good at it, you can do 200 by yourself. This carried on later to my other ministry roles and now into my work as the senior pastor of Oasis Church.

They might indeed do it differently for a short season. They may not do it as good. However, what I've found in many—if not most—cases is that since they can focus on one thing, they do it better. That's a lesson I had to learn as I equipped staff and lay leaders. I had to delegate, give the ministry away, and not try to be the superhero. At Oasis, we refer to this as the Jethro Principle. Check it out in Exodus 18.

8. **My church has given the okay; where do I go? What should I do? How do I afford it? What does my family do when I am away?**

Each one of these questions deserves a more in-depth answer. In future chapters, we will cover them in more detail. Still, establishing the pastor's sabbatical as a biblical practice—a God-given and blessed gift available to us—is not nearly as important as actually *deciding* to do so.

I am sure there are more questions and many more hesitations. We will examine some of these in the following chapters, but it's impossible to cover them all, as each person and situation is unique. We have covered some of the questions I have encountered, and I believe these will be helpful to you.

So, let's go! It is time to start planning. I would love to have you along as we explore the beautiful gift of the sabbatical your church has granted you.

4

Why Every Pastor Needs a Sabbatical

Not just every pastor needs a sabbatical, but every ministry and full-time leader does. However, for now, let us focus on the pastor. The pastor has some unique issues and roles that other staff members do not share, even though they may carry some of the same weight as the lead pastor. Still, I must be transparent in telling you that our church has not yet reached the point of granting sabbaticals to any staff members other than the senior and lead pastor, other full-time pastoral staff, and executive staff positions. We still have a way to go here. It has been discussed, and we were very close to instituting the policy right before COVID-19 hit. Everything's changed since then, so that has been put on hold for now–which I hope will be sooner rather than later!

I will say this, though: not all roles require the same amount of time away or sabbatical leave, so this can vary greatly in how it is done and afforded to various roles on the full-time team.

By now, there should not be any doubt that I believe *all* pastors should have some sabbatical leave, but it is not as simple as just saying, "We are sending you on sabbatical. Bye. See you in two or six months." No, there is a lot to consider and plan for. It might take a year or two to institute this in your church, but the sooner you get started, the better chance you will have to salvage a good pastor and keep them at your church longer.

There has been some mention of secular sabbaticals that might include educators, medical personnel, company executives, or select long-term employees of companies. It is surprising how long it has taken for the business world to begin to see the benefits. Still, they are responding rather quickly now that they see the long-term benefits for their employees and their bottom line as a company: to make money for the owner or the shareholders; so, they weigh everything very carefully. There are some well-known ones you will recognize that have sabbatical policies.

You might be surprised that the first large company to have a written formal sabbatical policy was McDonald's. Yes, the Big Mac, Ronald McDonald's. TIME[8] mentions they started this practice way back in 1977. Others[9] that reward their long-tenured team members with this gift are REI, Patagonia, Intel, The Cheesecake Factory, Quick Trip, The Container Store, Timberland, and several others. While some business statistics mention only around 16% percent offering sabbaticals[10], the percentage of large companies and corporations providing a form of sabbatical for some of their employees is as high as 50 percent. It is not just a religious thing. It is good business, too.

Now, making a case for the biblical sabbatical is obvious and straightforward. We have and will continue to do so throughout this book. However, a profit-centered company would never do this without an incentive (not just for the employee but also for the company.)

Michael Hyatt, the former CEO of Thomas Nelson Publishing, the largest Christian publisher in the world, mentions it in his case for sabbaticals[11]. Steven R. Covey, of the best-selling book *The Seven Habits of Highly Effective People* (Covey, May 19, 2020), said, "It is to sharpen the saw, to make their workers even more productive after a period of extended rest."[12]

D. J. DiDonna, who calls himself a social entrepreneur, along with Matt Boom, a "Well-being at Work" expert at the University of Notre Dame, set out to interview hundreds of people who had taken sabbaticals to discover their experiences, which he explains in his article "The Urgent Case for Sabbaticals for All." He had to take a self-induced sabbatical for the first time because he was burned out from his career and life. He then set out to learn more about sabbaticals, who take them, why, and the benefits of the sabbatical. In this, the first academic paper of our time, he says:

> Sabbaticals might be good for companies, too: We found that they increase employee satisfaction and retention and that people who were given sabbaticals by their employers returned more energized about their work with increased feelings of creativity and loyalty. Leaders who went on sabbatical came back

with new ideas, and a better understanding of what goes wrong—or well—in their absence.[13]

So, if you are a layperson reading this or a leader in your church contemplating sending your pastor on a sabbatical, maybe you should also consider this for yourself, your business, or your career. The same principles that nurture the employee's well-being apply in many ways to the secular workplace as they do to the sacred. The biblical benefits of restoration, increased feelings of creativity and loyalty, etc., can potentially benefit every organization that seeks to implement them. This book may be the start of your workplace considering sabbaticals or extended leaves of absence. You can look further into the various resources we have added at the end of this book and throughout our footnotes for additional information on this argument.

The title of this chapter asks the question: Why does every pastor need a sabbatical? Yes, what are the benefits of taking one? You might have noticed—or perhaps not—that few pastors who are often quoted have written much about sabbaticals, and there are relatively few books specifically addressing pastoral sabbaticals. It might be that not many pastors have taken them to write or talk about them. However, plenty of them talk about how tired they are. There are plenty of religious self-help books and books advising you on how to overcome this or that challenge, but sabbaticals have seen little coverage. I challenge you to find the current thinking from your denomination or the group of churches with which you fellowship. There are a few, but they are very few, especially in the type of conservative evangelical churches where I've pastored and have friends.

I am not sure if, in my circles, I have ever met a pastor who took a sabbatical as part of his church's policy. I knew of many unfortunate pastors who experienced forced "sabbaticals" due to burnout, physical issues, medical problems, moral failures, and other crises, but sadly, forced sabbaticals are not indeed a sabbatical. Call it what you may, and at the end of the day, hopefully, the pastor and church that suffer through this get the healing and restoration they need. But wouldn't it be so much better had we been more proactive in getting the time alone, rest, restoration, and spiritual re-energizing that a sabbatical brings instead?

Sadly, even most of the articles and blogs I have read, and some that I've quoted in this book, are told by those preaching about sabbaticals now, but would tell you their first sabbatical was a forced one because of something in the list above. If these pastors and their churches had made the proactive sacrifices it takes to establish a sabbatical policy and live it out, the pastor, the church, the pastor's family, and the many whom they influence in the larger community could have avoided many wounds and scars.

Okay, you may say: you've given us some good examples of the secular world doing what the spiritual world should be doing now. What about us? What about the church during your sabbatical?

Most of us have heard of senior faculty in higher education having sabbaticals as well as those in the medical research world. Still, the first sabbaticals in the United States were by a Christian college. Harvard, which most would agree is anything but a Christian beacon of light in our country today, started as a Christian university in 1636. They established the first sabbatical policy known in the late 1800s, "for the purpose of 'health, rest, study or the prosecution of original work in literature or science.'" (Hollis, 1962). There you have it: the biblical sabbatical began in our country based on Christian education and culture. While Harvard and other institutions like it have strayed from their Christian roots, the biblical principles have not changed, and neither have the health benefits that can be achieved through an effective sabbatical policy.

Michael Hyatt, on one of his Full Focus podcasts,[14] shared his experience of taking a sabbatical after leaving Thomas Nelson Publishing. Imagine the stress and pressure this CEO has been under for decades. He recounts his journey and struggles taking his first sabbatical. Now, he is probably the foremost voice in the Christian community promoting sabbaticals through Full Focus (formerly Michael Hyatt & Co.), a company he founded.

In his podcast, "I'm Going on a Sabbatical and You Should Too,"[15] Michael shares five key lessons he learned during his first sabbatical and what you should know. This is what, in a nutshell, he suggests a sabbatical helps you accomplish:

1. Recharge physically and emotionally.

2. Slow down and enjoy being.

3. Feed your spiritual side.

4. Get clarity on your priorities and goals.

5. Get on the same page as your spouse.

A lot can be said about each of these. My list is similar yet different from my context and role as a pastor. I encourage you to listen to or read anything Michael Hyatt has to say on this subject.

Here's another list from a church planter's sabbatical that he reluctantly took and lived to write about after thirteen years of inner-city church ministry. He is Michael Morgan, and he pastors the Wellspring Community Church in Aurora, Colorado. These are the benefits he found from taking a sabbatical from his article "What I Learned About Sabbaticals by Finally Taking One."[16] (You can check out the article for all the details at thegospelcoalition.org.):

- Sabbaticals teach us that we are more than what we achieve.
- Sabbaticals are a gift to the church.
- Sabbaticals are a gift to the whole family and not just the pastor.
- Sabbaticals are not a vacation.
- Sabbaticals require humility.
- Sabbaticals remind us that we can live without screens, the internet, and cell phones.
- Sabbaticals remind us of the joy of our calling.

Now, about my list . . .

I have already shared how the sabbatical leave policy came about in our church, Oasis Church of South Florida. My sabbatical was not forced like so many I have heard, but it came about just before I was at risk of unraveling.

Our church council is a group of men and women nominated and voted on by our congregation annually to counsel the pastor on matters related to our church. The church council sets my salary and oversees and approves our annual budget. They are my sounding board and the biggest blessing any leadership group could ever be. I don't know how I would have made it in one church (coming from a church planter to a thirty-four-year-old maturing church with many ministries) without having so many men and women who have supported me, challenged me, shared a common vision with me, imparted wisdom and more than anything, showed incredible patience with me. I am grateful. This group approved the sabbatical policy; they voted to give me a month each summer to prepare, study, and write as I'm doing now with this book.

They also embraced our crazy vision to give over $1 million to Haiti in ten years, a commitment that began in 2011 amid the biggest recession of my lifetime. They believed in the need to *love pastors* and *love cities* and led the way in instituting the ministry we call LCLP (Love Cities, Love Pastors). Our church has given well over $1 million to this initiative in the last ten years and established a pastoral retreat center called the Oasis Beach House, where hundreds of pastors have stayed at minimal to no cost to them or their families. These ministries do not directly benefit anyone in our church, but they do help serve thousands of Haitians and, now, several thousand pastors and their families.

Forgive me if I take a little side road to talk about these mature believers who saw the need and approved the gift of sabbaticals in my church. They have done so much more than that. Because of these members of our church council, I am able to write this book. I must give them credit for so much of the love we can share with pastors. Many are hurting, planting churches alone, and may need a cheerleader. I can only hope that if you are a pastor, your elders, church council, or the group of believers you're surrounded with are as much of a blessing to you in your ministry as the members of my own church council have been to me. And, if you are a lay leader, an elder, or a church council member, you are encouraged to know that much of what you approve of (or not) directly impacts your church's health. Sabbaticals are one of those.

Now, let's move on to my list of takeaways from my sabbatical journey. Again, this list is not exhaustive. The order is not from most important to least important. It may not be the same list you might have from your sabbatical experience, but it gets the discussion going.

1. A time to reflect.

In our day-to-day ministry, we are so busy that there is little time to reflect, yet we encourage our church to live in the simple faith: "Be still and know that I am God" (Psalm 46:10).

At times, I have stayed so busy and lived such a loud life that if the Holy Spirit wanted to speak to me, I couldn't hear Him. During one of my annual week-long prayer and fasting retreats, I remember walking on a path in the Great Smoky Mountains outside Gatlinburg, Tennessee. There I was, on a trail in the most visited national park in the United States, where—to the surprise of many—over 10 million people visit annually. Nope, I was not in Yellowstone or one of the famous ones out west but in the Great Smokies, where millions visit and find miles of trails and places to get alone and reflect. On this day, I was doing just that, reflecting. And in the scope of an hour, I received about twenty sermon ideas from what I observed on the trail. This level of intuitive thought does not normally occur (and hasn't since), but God was just pouring His thoughts to me that day—one sermon theme or core idea after another. I believe the only way I could have received them was that I was alone with Him, attentive to hearing Him, expectant to listen to His voice. I still have those ideas written down and haven't shared all of them yet, but it doesn't matter; they refueled me like nothing I could have planned. All this happened on a particular day I had set apart to reflect alone with God (imagine the possibilities with an extended time set aside for Him).

2. **A time to rest.**

Okay, I failed this test even on sabbatical. Sometimes, I believe I don't have it in me to rest. One thing we will discuss as we establish a sabbatical policy is that while we plan and set goals, in the end, nothing should prevent us from simply sitting somewhere and resting. Some guys can go fishing for weeks, go to the mountains and hunt, or sit on a beach for days without interruption. While I admire that and would love to do it, I can't. So, when I say *rest*, this is subjective.

One thing I can do is sleep in if I want. I can sit in my pajamas all day and just look at the mountains. I can read at will. I have a stack of books that I read, which I always have a half dozen or so I read at a time, with some I never finish. I am a bit crazy—I know. So, resting is not the same for all of us.

I work hard. I play hard. Then, I rest hard, but not always in the proper order. Just being away from the day-to-day ministry, where texts, calls, meetings, issues, problems, hurting people, and sermons are to be done by the weekend, is rest to me. Whew, I am tired just thinking about this. How so many pastors do this for years—even decades—and never take a sabbatical is beyond me now that I have experienced it. God was so gracious to get my attention before I crashed and burned.

(Maybe by reading this little book, God is trying to get your attention and saying to you: *stop, rest, and get away*. This is your sign!)

3. It restores my soul, my mind, and my body.

Psalms 23 is such a beautiful passage. We love to read it, but do we live it? How many have sat beside still waters for hours, maybe days, or walked through the beautiful valleys created by God and stood or hiked to the mountaintops to bask in His creation? Maybe on vacation? But that is always a sprint, though we usually do it with family or friends. There seems to be no time to be restored or to take in the beauty of Psalm 23. Vacations are needed. I'll keep saying it, but they can't take the place of extended times alone, away.

Most of what happens in my soul, mind, and body often goes unnoticed, both in the moment and in its aftermath. Its passing or impact might be subtle. But I found that spending extended time alone with God is essential. It is what truly recharges and restores me, preparing me for when I return to the pulpit. In ministry, chaos can quickly take over, and we need the margin to take the punches—and I mean real punches—from church members, council members, staff, and well . . . just life in ministry. Only after this uninterrupted communion with Jesus can we return with renewed focus on Him and His call to feed His sheep.

On my last sabbatical, our council allowed me to split it up as I've been at Oasis from the beginning, and our policy allows me to take six months. (I know it sounds extreme, and we will discuss that later, but don't try to do six months for your first one.) We had come through the pandemic, and there were so many unknowns and issues we were still maneuvering through as a church—I am sure our confusion about the safest way forward for ourselves and our congregations was not much different than what most church communities felt—so I asked the council if we could split the sabbatical up to four months and then two the following year. They agreed, even though I am generally not a proponent of splitting the sabbatical and would not usually recommend it.

In the scope of a few months around the pandemic, I had to remove a few of our most crucial pastoral team members from our team. One for moral impropriety and the other for dealing with marital issues. It was painful and hurtful to them, their families, our staff, our church, and me. Of course, as pastors, we can't always share with our congregation all the details on the "why," mainly to protect them and their confidentiality and confidence in ours, as well as having concern for the privacy of the people involved. Providing too much information can sometimes leave room for gossip, division, and questioning the leaders' motives and wisdom. I get it; it comes with the territory. Addressing these deeply personal issues that had threatened our church's mission was hard. It affected several of our staff, including a senior team member married to someone we had to move off our team. Then, add to the equation the pandemic, which, in a few ways, helped give some separation from that situation since we were all locked in, and no one was seeing anyone. When we returned, it was awkward sometimes since, in ministry, so many families are intertwined in the church. I took my sabbatical the following summer and was refreshed, restored, rested, and ready to hit the ground running . . . or so I thought.

On the first day back in the office after four life-changing months on a hard-won sabbatical, the spouse of a team member (whom I had let go before the pandemic) had asked for a divorce from my key executive. This wasn't just personal; I loved both of them dearly and had spent the last ten years working alongside them, sharing hundreds of hours in retreats and planning sessions. It was a gut punch. I ached for each of them, for our church family that didn't yet know, and for our staff. The weight of how this would affect our church and team, especially given their leadership roles, was overwhelming. We took time to work through the situation, and I witnessed God's grace in the life of the spouse who had been left. We tried our best to love and support them through this difficult time, even though it often felt like we weren't doing enough.

A month after getting the news of this dear family's split, I was away at the first conference I had attended in about three years, the first since the pandemic had begun. Tonia was with me, and it was all set to be a very special conference where all the guests had come by invitation only to this five-star hotel in Texas. I had looked forward to it. Then, on my first morning there, I got a call from our business manager with a message that said, "Please, call me right away." He never calls with this serious tone and does his best never to bother me when I'm away. From that call came one of the most bizarre and hurtful situations I had ever had with a staff member. We found out that years ago, a pastoral staff member committed a felony while pastoring in another state and had served time; however, he had not been truthful with us or his previous employers over the years. It was three months of investigations, lawyers, and pain. It ended in us having to terminate, probably the most beloved pastor on our staff and, very possibly, the most beloved pastor in our church in the thirty-four years of Oasis Church's history. The pain and the hurt it caused everyone, including him and his dear family, and so many who respected him and loved him, were like none I had experienced. Through each of these experiences, we lost good and faithful families, some of whom had been with us for years. They could not separate the situation from the person and why they had to leave, so these families left the church. I don't have to tell you, pastor, how that hurts. You know. It's devastating. Regardless of how many you've lost over the years, how big your church is, or how long you've been in ministry, you are a shepherd, and losing one of your sheep hurts deeply, regardless of why.

Now, if I share these two difficult stories (which were also shared with our entire church, as they involved high-impact, visible leaders and teachers), it is to illustrate the difficult paths pastors must sometimes navigate in ministry. Had I not taken my sabbatical after a terrible pandemic experience, I don't believe I would have survived. I probably would not have stayed in ministry. It was deeply painful, hurtful, and draining, all while trying to love those who were hurt and nurse our church back to health after a six-month shutdown due to COVID-19.

Later, I thanked our church council—who had been aware of what was going on the whole time—for approving sabbaticals, and I shared with them that if I had not taken my sabbatical, I would not have made it through this time. After returning from my extended time away, I had the margin to take the arrows, the gut punches, the questioning, and all that goes with these seasons, which only those of you who are pastors understand. That sabbatical was a godsend beyond what I can say. That alone was worth all the sacrifices and planning over the years that laid the foundation for me to be able to take sabbaticals.

It saved my ministry.

Around the same season, we also lost a young pastor to a national ministry. I had encouraged him to take this opportunity; however, with him and the previous three senior team members gone, we had lost all our pastoral, teaching, and executive team from the pandemic's beginning until the end, except for one other member and me. Yes, 80 percent of our senior leadership team was gone. But now, as I look back, I can only praise God, who brought us new team members for a fresh season. And well, that young pastor I mentioned, pastor Alex Rivera, the one who left for another wonderful ministry? He eventually rejoined our staff as our Executive Pastor. Not only that, but as this book is being published, Pastor Alex Rivera has been ordained and voted in to be Co-Pastor alongside me. In 2-3 years, he will step into the role of Lead Pastor. Only God could have orchestrated all of this–certainly not me. A new wind is blowing, and we are seeing growth at Oasis Church, both numerically and spiritually, like we have not seen in decades.

If I had not had the sabbatical season for rest and getting refreshed, I would not have experienced this new season and had a front-row seat to witness what God is doing in our midst. I am confident I would have just retired. I am at the age I could have, and trust me . . . it crossed my mind. Why do I share this raw and real pain that our church and I experienced? It is because every pastor has or will experience something similar or worse, and if you are running on empty and have not had the time to get healthy, you will *not* survive a Cat-5 hurricane. That is why I am so passionate about taking sabbaticals.

4. I can do what I never get to do.

Many pastors long to have certain hobbies but can't. Why? Because of their schedules. Many dream of returning to getting that degree or finishing a doctorate. Perhaps they will write a book or further their education in a particular field. Pastors are people, too. They want to enjoy life and live it to its fullest, as it is said; yet we find ourselves on the proverbial "rat wheel" racing around when, before we know it, we look up, and the kids are grown, and we never got to do what we'd dreamed of. This might sound selfish, but it is the truth. Pastors are people. They are not machines, nor are they robots. You can't wind pastors up and just let them go. It does not work that way.

I'm sorry if it is selfish. Too many pastors leave the ministry to have some free time, time to rest, and time for family and a normal life. Yes, we commit our lives to the ministry and to God. Yes, we follow a call. We should be 100 percent sold out to this calling, but we are human. If ministry were so easy, there would not be a soon-to-be critical shortage of pastors. If ministry were so easy and fun, people would be lining up to attend seminary and become pastors. I don't see them lined up at my door saying, "I want into this calling." No, it's a God-calling, and as I told my boys while they were kids, I will never ask, expect, or push you to ministry. It's a calling; if you are not called when those times I described in the last section come, you will quit, burn out, and turn away from the church and often from the Lord.

Sabbaticals allow for some freedom to explore not only geographically but in all kinds of ways. During my first sabbatical, I fully restored and remodeled a two-bedroom cabin in the Smokies, which we'd bought and rented out in Gatlinburg, Tennessee, for years. It was hard work; I dropped into bed almost every night exhausted, but it was something that I usually don't do and can't do. It helped me through the first sabbatical of withdrawing from my beloved church, which I had not left for fifteen years. That cabin kept me so occupied for the first six weeks that it was the best thing I could do that first time. On another sabbatical, I oversaw the rebuilding of that same cabin that was burned in the 2016 wildfires, which destroyed 2,000 cabins and homes in Gatlinburg, Tennessee. Then, on another sabbatical, I remodeled another house for a month. No, I wouldn't say I *like* remodeling, and I'm terrible at it, but it is very cathartic.

On two sabbaticals, I did long bike rides. I took a month from one sabbatical and rode from Miami to New York City on a bike (no, not a motorcycle) that you pedal a million strokes. I raised the initial $158,000 toward our Haiti missions through donations and pledges. On another sabbatical, I spent two months riding my bike from San Diego, California, back to Miami, covering all 3,000 miles, to raise an additional half-million dollars for Haiti. Now, those sabbaticals don't sound too restful physically and mentally. I concede they were not, but the other benefits outweighed the sacrifice. It was my time; I could do whatever I wanted. I chose to drive this old body for all it had in it, daily, to fulfill a commitment to our orphanage, schools, and churches in Haiti. That was refreshing and renewing spiritually for me. But I'll admit again, I am a bit *"cray, cray,"* as they say. I don't recommend you do any of these. You have your own bucket list or passion that you can't do on vacation or a day off. But you can do things you could only dream of during a sabbatical.

On another sabbatical, I was a chaplain on a ten-day Mediterranean cruise and took Tonia. A short trip like that could not fit into my regular schedule. I've visited Greece and studied Paul's missionary journeys, visited friends and relatives I would not usually get to see, and it goes on and on. Yes, I do some spiritual things and occasionally visit other churches. And I also, Lord forbid, sleep in on some Sundays and do not go anywhere because I worship online.

5. Re-evaluate goals, life stage, and plan.

Again, this is voluntary since it is not something that has to be done. It is on the list of things I have done, and some readers may want to do. Many people taking business sabbaticals make this re-evaluation a significant part of their experience.

We are not asked to plan for our future as part of our job description, but envisioning and planning are some things I have done, and you may also want to consider doing so. You would notice that many people who take business sabbaticals make planning for the different stages of life a big part of their extended time of rest.

My first sabbatical was for three months. As I mentioned earlier, I spent the first six weeks remodeling our cabin in the mountains and then spent three weeks in the Mediterranean, serving as a chaplain on a cruise and touring Italy. Being a chaplain is not offered much anymore; however, most of us can't do those things regularly. I still have opportunities to serve as a chaplain for a week on cruises worldwide, yet almost all of them coincide with Christmas or Easter weeks. Uh, no. I am a pastor of a church, and those two weeks are generally the two most heavily attended in the year. Most of us can't get away for those weeks, but it would be appropriate if you were on a sabbatical during that time. Planning is critical. So far, I haven't been able to make that work for the round-the-world cruise. There is little you can do as a cruise chaplain (who needs or wants spiritual advice on a cruise?), but a few want a Sunday service.

So, three months went by rather quickly, and I did a lot of dreaming about the next three, five, ten, and twenty years. I remember distinctly thinking about my sabbatical after fifteen years when I'd turn sixty-five. I'd spend time praying and thinking about how long I'd continue to pastor. At fifty years old, I had so much left to do and so much vision; I still think it was (and is) enough for two more lifetimes. At sixty, the temptation was to consider my future and retirement from full-time pastoring. Many of my fellow friends in the ministry and other pastors my age were already planning, and some were already announcing it. I was about sixty when people began asking me about retirement. I continued to say, "I would look at it at sixty-five during my sabbatical." But I had seen so many—even guys on our staff in their fifties—already talking about retirement, who then got distracted. Distractions when planning for retirement come quickly when you are in the full swing of ministry, especially when you are younger, and that season seems to be still so far away.

Yes, we need to plan for retirement. However, my financial preparation for retirement was rather mediocre during my younger years as a church planter. After leaving behind a good salary from the church, I went to start Oasis (with three younger boys approaching adolescence); it was all we could do to pay the bills and survive, much less putting aside extra money for a retirement that seemed so distant still. I am now playing catch-up, big time. While I had prepared for many long-term financial aspects, setting aside time to plan for actual retirement early on was not easy, as distractions abounded.

Some of the guys I served with and knew in ministry left, never returned, and essentially retired. I think that if they had a sabbatical to look forward to every five or so years, they, along with many other pastors, would have stayed in ministry well into their senior years, when their experience and wisdom could be of value to their church and the younger generation preparing to take the baton from them. Again, the lack of sabbaticals can even affect retirement and the preparation of the next generation of pastors who will take on the churches we serve. Instead, senior leaders and lead pastors must go it alone and try to end the race maybe earlier than they would have. There are so many advantages to a sabbatical—they are almost endless.

At sixty-five, the sabbatical was finally here to do what I knew had to be dealt with. I prayed and wrestled; honestly, it was easier than I thought because the pandemic changed everything. (Another reason why more pastors are leaving the ministry and suffering mental and physical challenges than ever before.) It pushed me to verbalize how long I can lead. Following that sabbatical, although I did not have a specific date or plan, I knew God had given me peace, indicating that it would be sooner rather than later, and would probably begin around seventy or so, not eighty to ninety years old, as some pastors are pastoring today. I have shared this with our council and said a little to our church. (Update: The dates, timeline, and next lead pastor have now been decided, and our church has voted on them since I first started writing this book.) I am passionate about not holding back the future of Oasis Church because of my lack of stamina or ability to continue leading at the level I have for many years. It is time to pass the baton to the next generation in three to five years.

Will I retire and move to the mountains? Many think I will, but I do not think so. I love South Florida, and I love the mountains. But only God knows what the future brings. I am reminded of the book of James, in the fourth chapter, verses 13–16, which tells us we do not know what tomorrow brings, in humility to trust the Lord, and as He wills, we will live day by day. A perfect reminder to plan, but . . . plan with a pencil and eraser, so when God decides, we are willing to change and erase our plans for His plans. I never plan to retire from ministry because I do not believe *retirement* is in the Bible, especially for a calling to ministry. But the Bible does tell us that various seasons are normal. I hope to remain actively involved in local church ministry and international ministry. If Oasis allows me to have some part in our Love Cities, Love Pastors, or Bike for Haiti initiatives, or other areas, then that would be wonderful. But if that is not God's will, I know He will provide a ministry. I hope to always have a ministry to pastors, even if it is just taking them to coffee or sitting by the pool at our Oasis Beach House, listening to their journeys and struggles in both their private lives and public ministry, since pastors often have no one they can talk to or who can understand. So, sabbaticals have given me time and space to pray, think, plan, and dream, not only about the vision for Oasis but even for my future. That is just hard to do in our day-to-day ministry. Often, abrupt leaves "for personal reasons," such as family troubles or stress-related illnesses, are made on the spur of the moment, out of emotion, or following a traumatic season in ministry. Sabbaticals help us clear our heads and hearts, hear from God, and talk to Him about the future.

As a side note, the words I first spoke when starting this book have now evolved into a Pastoral Succession Plan for myself and Oasis Church. We are currently implementing a two-year succession plan. You can learn more about this plan and how it works in our new book, which I initially wrote for our church leadership and shared with our congregation. Since 90% of churches lack a succession plan in place, I have decided to make it available to a wider audience in a small book on Amazon, available in both paperback and eBook editions. Just look for the *Pastoral Succession Plan* by Guy Melton. I believe it could be a helpful resource.

Okay, back to re-evaluating life. Of course, when I was younger, I could come back with many long-term plans, so much so that my staff, after my first sabbatical, began to dread my return because they knew it would be much more work for them. LOL, and it usually has been.

The seeds for almost every major event or ministry that Oasis has undertaken (and we have undertaken some major ones for a church our size in South Florida, one of the most unchurched regions of the country) have emerged during a sabbatical or one of my annual prayer and fasting retreats. God has used every one of them over the last twenty years. It grieves me to think of the pastor who does not get to have the space for God to speak and give them big dreams because they have no margin in their calendar to dream and plan. After reading this book, I pray that someone will make the time and space for God's inspiration to make their call flourish.

6. Focus on family, personal issues, and life challenges.

Sabbaticals have the potential to enrich your life and your family's. This cannot be emphasized enough. Focus on the season you find yourself in. Pastors raising kids cannot take them along, cannot leave a wife with the kids for extended periods, and cannot get away for three or six months at a time. That is obvious—I hope. Creative thinking and planning are essential for every stage, but they can be accomplished. (More on that in a later chapter about planning for your sabbatical.) However, sabbaticals can be an expanded time with the family, more than the traditional vacation, racing to and from somewhere in a week.

A sabbatical allows a husband and wife to spend extended time together that they never get, either because of raising a family or having little ones at home, accompanied by the rigors of ministry. This doesn't mean that marriage doesn't take constant work. It does. Just taking a sabbatical will not heal a broken marriage. But this is the icing on the top of the cake, to get that extra time together, as I have mentioned, on cruises and trips to other countries while on sabbaticals. I must clarify that Tonia and I do not spend most of our time together while I am on sabbatical. She likes her space and would not dream of riding a bike or even following one cross-country, camping for two months, or remodeling cabins, you get what I mean. So, we have strategically planned things for our time together, but it is not a major part of my sabbatical, yet we have the freedom that we do not usually get to plan and do something, even on the spur of the moment.

We have taken our grandsons on a trip across the country as we did with their parents when they were younger. It was one of the best times of my life. I will never forget it. We have taken all the grands on special trips and have the freedom to drop in on their regular lives, which is something pastors don't usually do because we are working on Sundays when everyone else is off. Do I hear any amens? Yes, I even get to do some 'honey-do' list items during the sabbatical, even though I never finish as many as Tonia wants or as many as are needed. Now, I am getting convicted . . .

Another aspect is not only spending quality family time but also for personal enrichment. With so much pressure today and the stigma of mental illness and burnout happening in our society, many pastors need counseling or coaching in their personal lives. Extended times allow space to work on issues that are sometimes so serious they have the potential to negatively impact their ministry and marriage, or maybe even push them over the edge if the case is extreme. Many pastors would not think of reaching out to someone in town, but on sabbatical, you can plan to be ministered to by someone outside your area. Some need specific health issues to be addressed that have been put off, while others need to focus on achieving a healthy weight. It will take some time to get their lives in order and balance their diet and exercise. Sabbaticals are a good time for that, too. Oh no, I just said the dirty word . . . *exercise*. Sorry. But honestly, exercise may be one of the greatest needs for a pastor. Exercise is like a mini-sabbatical from everything else that needs to be a part of our lives. I know I've gone into preaching now, but I wouldn't say I like it; yet, I know how much it renews me and helps me during the most stressful and busy times. Ok, I'll stop now.

5

Isn't Vacation Enough? What's the Difference?

What is the difference between taking a vacation and a sabbatical? This is one of the most asked questions when sabbaticals come up. I have given this much thought and wrestled with it, even after taking multiple sabbaticals for almost twenty years. Believe it or not, I still wrestle with this question. There is no perfect answer or one-size-fits-all solution—just as you'll come to realize if you haven't yet, about nearly every aspect of the sabbatical. Each person and organization are unique, making it difficult to write a book where everyone fits into a single template. No, it is not that easy, and if you think this book will solve and answer all the questions you and your church might have, you will be disappointed as well.

My purpose is to offer an argument for the sabbatical discussion and get the subject out there to be considered because I believe the rhythms of rest and renewal are as important a part of the ministry for a pastor as any other. Not only that but I am also convinced that a sabbatical is an integral part of *every aspect* of ministry.

So, what is a sabbatical? Simply put, it is an extended time away. Now, isn't that easy? Oh, I wish it were that easy.

To distinguish between a vacation and a sabbatical, we want to offer some simple clarifications that many who have never experienced a sabbatical may not understand.

Sadly, for many pastors, finding or making the time and having the finances for a long-week vacation is challenging enough. Unfortunately, even some pastors reading this right now have not taken a vacation in years.

But leaping into this big assumption that we all take vacations, you may ask: What makes a vacation different from a sabbatical?

A vacation is a limited time away determined by the organization, whether a business or a church. Most churches give time away and call it a vacation when a pastor or staff person gets to take a break from work. It might be a week for short-tenured staff or even up to five or six weeks for pastors who have been in ministry for twenty-five or more years.

A vacation is for relaxation. It is about enjoyment and recreation. It is for family events, travel, and anything leisurely. The average vacation is a week or two, even if someone has more time. Many churches only allow a certain amount of time away, so in our case, two weeks is the most a person can be away for a vacation simultaneously. Most pastors and staff I know take a vacation for a week and, at most, sometimes, in two-week increments.

This is where the sabbatical and vacation vary significantly. Yes, a vacation might be restful and fun, but then again, depending on how far you go and what you do. It might be like how I do vacation: I must do something else to get rested when I get home from it. A vacation for me has always been to drive as far as you can and do as much as you can cram into one week or two.

As a young dad, I had hoped someday to take my family on a nationwide vacation visit and drive across the country and back. From South Florida and the tip of the U.S. to the great Northwest, it is approximately 3500 miles each way. For example, years ago, I made that trip with my oldest son, who now lives in Seattle, Washington, when he first moved out there. We did it in six days and in July in an old blue Dodge without A/C that a retired lady in our church had given him. Yes, mid-summer. I will leave it at that. While I had to take a week of vacation to do it, it was not the usual vacation. When we arrived in Seattle, they had three days of weather over 100 degrees Fahrenheit, which I believe was record heat. We tent-camped, and while we sweated in record temps with no A/C in the car during the day, it was in the high thirties at night (this South Floridian froze on the tent floor.) So, that's to give you an idea of how I take *vacations*.

Years before that, when my kids were younger, myself, my three boys, and Tonia took a road trip from Hollywood, Florida all the way to the Adirondacks of New York, sleeping in our old pop-up camper every night. We pulled it to New York City and even visited the old Shea Stadium for a Mets baseball game. Yes, I drove a pop-up camper through the streets of Manhattan.

What a ridiculous and foolish thing to do. And I also called *that* a vacation. We were so tired after driving for twenty nights up and down the East Coast and stopping at every major city along the way that on our last night, as we approached Central Florida, I said to Tonia, "We do have a campground spot for this last night, but what do you think of just driving on home?" Yep, it didn't take a prayer or time to let me think about it. She said, "Let's do it." And so, we did. We crashed when we arrived home. That was not a restful or leisurely vacation, to say the least, even though it was three weeks. But we traveled up and down the East Coast, and my dream of exploring it with my family was realized.

I will "land the plane," as my wife tells me, after sharing with you The Big Kahuna of vacations: the West Coast trip. 8,000 miles in three weeks in a rented minivan. Yes, coast to coast and back. How? Well, let us say it wasn't restful or leisurely either. To spare most of the gory details and yet clarify the difference between a sabbatical and a vacation, I must tell it. Or more like, I want to tell you. Ha!

Twenty-one days with a high school teenager, a middle school teen, and a nine-year-old who had more energy than was needed to lift a rocket into space. My lifelong dream: taking my family on this trip. Up to that point, we had rarely taken a vacation; I don't think I ever remember more time away than a few nights at a campground. So obviously, having never traveled and seen the beautiful country we live in, I wanted my boys to experience more.

How would you do a three-week vacation if you were me? You drive all day, and when you get to a tourist attraction or landmark you want to see, you stop for an hour and then get back in the car. Yes, we did that. We did it at the Alamo in Texas for one hour and at the Grand Canyon for an hour and a half. We stayed in Las Vegas for cheap food and a cheap motel, and then headed out. San Francisco was a drive-through; there was no time to stop. We splurged and stayed overnight in Yosemite in a tent, which gave us a ten-hour visit there. And on and on it went for twenty-one days. Mostly driving, sleeping, and eating, and just like that, we were back home. But we had seen the whole United States of America. Another dream was realized. My sons complained the whole time; my youngest lost every bit of his spending money daily because he misbehaved and drove his brothers nuts in the van. Remember, we didn't have any phones with apps; we had no Gameboys, Switches, or handheld gaming devices back then. Oh, my poor wife. What Tonia has put up with in our *fifty* years of marriage requires her to be a saint, and she is one for sure. We survived, and the boys said they hated it. Do you know what their favorite memories of growing up are now? The trip out west and the camping trip up the East Coast. Mission accomplished. Now, *that* is a vacation!

If you are wondering what is so restful about that? That is my point; this precious time off is not to rest but to sightsee, have fun, and do some recreational activities. Perhaps you could also visit relatives and stay in one spot. But that has its drawbacks, too—been there, done that. I'll spare you.

A vacation has a very short shelf life and is seldom restful and renewing. When I am on vacation, usually about halfway to three-quarters in, I think about what I must do when I return, how much I will be behind, and how long it will take me to catch up. I think of the house issues I've left undone, which now need to be done if I get a day off soon. You get my point. Vacations are great and necessary, but they are not a sabbatical and cannot be a stand-in for the long haul. Take vacations, yes, they are great. But they cannot take the place of a sabbatical.

Sabbaticals are an extended time away from work and are usually paid. They take planning and preparation. They typically have several goals related to your personal life, well-being, and ministry. A sabbatical gives you time to decompress, time to unwind, and renew your mind, heart, and soul. Sabbaticals are to restore your mental, physical, spiritual, and emotional life. They also provide the time that is usually not taken or cannot be squeezed into a busy ministry and life to read the books you haven't gotten to, learn new things, attend a class, write a book, and rest.

This chapter will not discuss all you can do on a sabbatical; we will address that later.

A sabbatical should benefit you, your church, and your ministry. A vacation is strictly for you and your family to get away for a much-deserved and earned season of play.

A sabbatical takes time. It cannot be rushed and can't have too many goals and expectations, or it will not do you any good. A sabbatical should have fun, family, and everything a vacation has, but it should not be considered a vacation. This is a huge point that every pastor and their church leadership must understand.

Another key point to consider is that vacations are yearly occurrences, typically lasting one to six weeks per year, depending on the organization and your staff status; however, this is not the case for sabbaticals. The Bible speaks of sabbaticals as a multi-year cycle, occurring every seventh year. Or as in the case of Oasis Church, every 5 years. I believe that most churches and businesses that offer sabbaticals understand this distinction: sabbatical time does not replace vacation. So, as our church does, I strongly recommend that whoever takes a sabbatical also take their vacation at another time during the year.

6

I Would Rather Burn Out Than Rust Out

It sounds so noble, doesn't it? *I'd rather burn out than rust out.* After all, the Bible instructs us to work hard. It tells us to get up early, work for our wages, and be responsible. The Bible talks about a worthy hire in many places, which typically implies a hard worker. Hard work is not just noble; it is biblical. In many places, Scripture tells us the importance of tending the fields and being willing to get up early and work until sunset. After all, farming and agricultural life in the Old and New Testament days was the norm (even up until 100 years ago, it was the norm for most families in the United States). Farming is hard work. It is not for the lazy, and Scripture again tells us a lazy man who does not plant, water, and work in his fields will have no crop and will be poor and starve (Proverbs 20:4). It says a man who does not feed his family is worse than an infidel (1 Timothy 5:8). You get it. The Bible very clearly instructs us to work hard.

As a pastor and ministry leader, I believe it is vital to honor the biblical call to responsibly tend the fields and flocks entrusted to us. We are called to serve those in our care with love and diligence, doing all things as unto the Lord. This includes setting aside time to pray, plan, and study for teaching His Word, making hospital visits, serving the poor, equipping the saints, and overseeing His church with integrity. Furthermore, it is essential to uphold the standard of being above reproach (1 Timothy 3:2) in every area of ministry. We are called to the most incredible and honorable role I can imagine. I sometimes pinch myself to think that God has allowed me to be in full-time ministry for almost 50 years. How can I not want to work as hard as I can with gratitude and appreciation for all He has done for me? However, Scripture tells us that . . .

> By the seventh day God had finished the work he had been doing; so on the seventh day he rested from all of his work. Then God blessed the seventh day and made it holy, because on it he rested from all the work of creating that he had done. (Genesis 2:2–3)

If God rested (and He didn't need to do it as the Creator of the universe), then it begs the question, why should we think it is better to "burn out than to rust out"? In the college I attended in the generation before me, it was taught almost as a theological doctrine by some pastors and leaders that "burning out" for God was spiritual and God's will for every pastor. Yes, this happened. I know most of you reading this are younger and—praise God—most have not heard this saying or had it laid on you as spiritual dogma to live by. Yet most of us as pastors live this out without saying it or even believing it. It is often sincere and stems from a genuine desire to please God, and oh yeah, to please our congregations. Of course, they want us to work hard . . . so hard that they will not even notice generally when we are about to burn out or melt down—that is, until it's too late. I am so thankful for the laymen and women leaders who watch after their pastors and not only pray for them but ensure they are given the honor that the apostle Paul in 1 Timothy 5 tells us is accorded to those undershepherds called to lay down their lives for the sheep: "The elders who direct the affairs of the church well are worthy of double honor, especially those whose work is preaching and teaching" (1 Timothy 5:17).

Paul describes our calling as a 'noble one' earlier in that same pastoral letter: "Here is a trustworthy saying: Whoever aspires to be an overseer desires a noble task" (1 Timothy 3:1). You are called to a great and noble role within the kingdom of God. It is humbling to read these verses and imagine their meaning for you and me, such imperfect (often unseen, unappreciated, and overworked) pastors and ministry staff.

The sad truth is that while our church may say 'amen' to these verses and nod their heads, most do not even realize they are a part of our burnout and failures, often without knowing, seeing, or understanding the unique needs of pastors and spiritual leaders. If you, as a pastor, can get this book into the hands of the most influential leaders in your church (whatever their role), then they can no longer claim ignorance of the needs of their pastor. I'm convinced that 99 percent of leaders who love God lead with a heart for their church. And they must know that the Lord will want to help keep their pastors healthy.

Still, we see the following headlines repeatedly, which seem to be becoming more the rule than the exception these days. (These are just a few headlines and stories I've read, but I know hundreds more like these.)

D.C. Megachurch Pastor Howard John Wesley announces Sabbatical on "Megachurch Pastor Steps Away from Pulpit Because He Feels Far from God, Tired in Soul."[17]

This is on Pastor Jim Burgen, "Flatirons Community Church Pastor on Why He Needs a Break."[18]

And, "Texas megachurch pastor Matt Chandler steps down after DMs with woman 'crossed a line.'"[19]

Not only that, other articles point to record numbers of pastors who are considering quitting as these show:

> "Yet another study confirms: Many pastors are hanging on by a thread."[20]

> "Hillsong founder Brian Houston steps down as leader of church"[21]

> "Rob Bell Not the First Megachurch Pastor to Step Down"[22]

These are only a handful of headlines of pastors stepping down and out of ministry due to affairs, malfeasance, burnout, immorality, mental and emotional breakdowns, and stress getting too much to bear. There are a hundred reasons, yet I believe most lead back to one factor: they got disconnected from God.

This sounds awful, and yes, it is frightening if you are a pastor, or a family member or friend of a pastor. Pastoral burnout has become almost an epidemic, and since the COVID-19 pandemic, it has become worse. The number of pastors stepping down is in the hundreds every month, adding up to thousands each year.

Every situation, church, and pastor is unique. Yet I have come to believe strongly that much of the cause for this problem begins with the "hero" or "Superman" syndrome that pastors get stuck in. Their ego often gets involved, and they feel guilty for not doing enough or not succeeding in their own eyes and those of others. It's just a vicious spiral to the bottom to find themselves disconnected from The True Vine that supplies life (John 15).

Whether you call it burnout or any other term, it is real, and the lack of healthy pastors is destroying families, lives, and churches.

Michael Morgan, pastor of Wellspring Community Church in Aurora, Colorado, put it this way: "Church planting was harder than I had ever dreamed and eight years into it, after meager results, I had become not only depleted but also skeptical of my calling. If my value is proportional to the size of this ministry, then I clearly wasn't worth much."[23]

This statement could be said by thousands of U.S. pastors right this minute. They may not say it out loud, but they feel it, which weighs on them daily.

Going back to my college days and the "*burn out versus rust out*" phrase so many used during that time, brings to mind several hundred of what the college called "preacher boys." Those who were called into the ministry of pastoring. We sat in endless classes on Theology and Doctrine and learned how to build a bigger, better church. Professors even predicted how big a church we would build and pastor. The sky was the limit. I think everyone dreamed of building churches in the thousands because that is what was told to us. Though neither they nor we recognized it at the time, the seeds of burnout and dropout were being planted.

The cost of a 24-hour-a-day ministry, year after year, takes a toll on your psyche, heart, soul, and body. I can't describe all this entails or everything I've dealt with in my years of pastoring Oasis Church. However, the burden of those broken individuals, marriages, families, the sick, the terminal, and the needy can sometimes be too much to bear.

Everyone wants a piece of you: text messages at all hours of the day and night, private messages, unscheduled appointments, and meetings. This does not include studying every week for multiple Sunday services and preparing for events. It does not include planning, visioning, reading, studying, and mastering the hundreds of details required to keep a church running in the twenty-first century. You not only have to be a shepherd today but a CEO. No human can stand this pressure for years without breaking under its weight. But "it's a noble calling," they tell us. *So . . . What do we do?*

This is why I make the case for sabbaticals. This is why I led Oasis Church to begin the Love Cities, Love Pastors ministry—which encourages, supports, and comes alongside church planters and inner-city pastors. And why the vision of our 365-days-a-year Oasis pastoral retreat center, called Oasis Beach House on Hollywood Beach, was brought to life.

My heart is broken for the many pastors I did not just read about, but also the ones I know personally who have left the ministry broken, disillusioned, or just simply crushed, if not physically ill. Each came into the ministry with a call. They came in with visions of helping the sick and the hurt, loving people, saving the lost, and making a difference, yet they dropped out defeated and wondering what had happened. Why?

It has been said that for every ten young pastors who go into ministry, only one completes their tenure and retires. Nine out of ten will drop out along the way. I used to question that. I do not anymore.

Years ago, I began to beg God to allow me to finish well. My pastor, Dr. V. S. Ackerman, did, and he constantly encouraged me and his other preacher boys to "not dip your colors,"[24] "don't mess up," and to "finish well." I do it not for my mentor but for Him, who called me. I have moments of fear that I might not finish well, even though I'm so close to the goal line in my ministry season. As they say in Football language, I'm not just deep in the fourth quarter but the "2-minute drill."

One day, as I challenged myself with the 1:10 ratio of dropout pastors, I began to count all the guys I graduated with and who went into ministry at the same time I did. To my shock and disappointment, I am the only one I could think of still pastoring a church. This breaks my heart. These are good men with big goals who loved God, but they left the pastoral ministry for a variety of reasons.

Are you still trying to figure out the *why* of this book? Why the trouble? Why the cost and time? If I can help save one pastor's life and ministry by showing them the value of a sabbatical, and help your church leaders understand its vital importance, then it is all worth it. My heart breaks daily when another statistic happens and another pastor burns out long before he rusts out.

I'm much more concerned about burnout than rusting out, and I hope you and your church leaders are, too.

7

Give Him a Sabbatical or Lose Him

(A Message to Church Leadership)

I am certain that by now, *you*, the church (lay or staff) leader responsible for making decisions on staff or church policy, agree that sabbaticals are biblical and necessary. However, you might need to consider some other reasons to help others see why it is important to gift your pastor an extended leave after a certain number of years—three, five, seven, or more. One of the greatest hindrances to sabbaticals in churches is getting the congregation and some leaders to appreciate the role of their pastor and how unique it is. Most pastors are even afraid to ask, knowing there will be resistance, which could make them look lazy.

I want to share a few key points that I believe every leader in the local church should be aware of. I'm sure you and your team can come up with more.

He Needs It

Your pastor may not even want one. He might be a workaholic, be wracked with guilt at the thought of taking time off or feel genuinely like he can't leave his flock for more than a week or so. However, he needs this time, even if he does not recognize it. Thankfully, some churches love and care for their pastors so much that they initiate discussions about a sabbatical before the pastor mentions it or is on their radar. Sadly, churches sometimes must force their pastor to accept a sabbatical because they see the need before he does.

The story below is the story of one man, but it can also be the story of thousands. In a video, Pastor Jim Burgen, the Pastor of Flatirons Community Church in Colorado, shared he was taking a sabbatical, not because he wanted one but because his leadership was making him.

> "Every time we turn on the news, it's like one more pastor fell apart," said Burgen. "[The elders] loved me so much that before there's a moral failure, before there's a financial failure, before there's all this list of things that have taken leaders out, they said, "Let's get on the front end of that and let's take you out and let you rest for six months and disconnect from Flatirons, so that I can come back."[25]

He went on a sabbatical because, at one of their last meetings, the elders told him he was exhausted and needed time away from the church.

"I'll be honest with you," said Burgen. "It felt more like an intervention than a loving confrontation."

While his first reaction was to resist what they were saying, viewing needing a break as a weakness, the elders persisted. And as Burgen considered his time at Flatirons over the past couple of years, he realized his elders were right.

Praise God for godly leaders who truly lead and confront the difficult issues. However, this is not common in the church. Most might be intimidated by the pastor or afraid of what others might think. But these elders might have saved their pastor, his marriage, and his pastorate at one of the largest churches in America. It shows that sabbaticals benefit not just pastors of small churches who are going solo in ministry but also those leading large churches and everything in between.

If you are a leader, you don't have to force your pastor into a sabbatical. If he's resistant, try sitting down for a heart-to-heart talk. I'm pretty sure any pastor reading this book wishes you would do so and would be glad if you did—he may just be afraid to talk about it.

Let Him or Lose Him

In earlier chapters, I said to the pastor how neglecting this biblical extended time away can cut short his ministry's life or impact. Now I'm speaking to you, *the church*: you will lose him. Whether it's burnout, meltdown, or worse, he may take a sabbatical in dire times, but it won't be called one. Most likely, he will take some time away to go somewhere else.

He won't tell you this. He won't say, "I am leaving since you won't give me an extended leave." That would make him look weak or lazy. But you will lose him. I have decades of proof to show how often pastors leave. Now, he may leave even if you give him a sabbatical. It is not a foolproof idea that a pastor who gets a sabbatical and is treated well by the church won't leave if God calls him to. He might still face burnout or struggle with life's many challenges. He's still human. However, a sabbatical can be a loving expression and an acknowledgment of his value to you and the church.

I can think of very few things that adequately show love and appreciation more than giving your pastor a sabbatical. In the short term, we may all prefer a raise or other perks. But in the twenty-first century, there is nothing better and more valuable than time.

The younger generations agree. Studies show that young millennials and Gen Zers value time off and away from the office more than money. Chances are high that you will encounter this in your church, if you haven't already. The next generations will want and need a sabbatical more than anything. You can show appreciation for them and their families by proactively providing time away before it is needed, forced, or they simply leave.

Pay Me Now or Pay Me Later

It is uncomfortable to mention so many things that deal with the harsh realities of our day. Money, mental illness, and personal and family crises are just realities of daily life, and this goes for pastors, too.

A church that does not pay its pastor a livable salary and take care of their essential needs is not a Christ-honoring church. That's harsh to say, but remember this:

In 1 Timothy 5:17–18, the Bible states the pastor is worthy of his hire and is to be cared for. Verse 17 says he is worthy of double honor. You can check whatever translation you like; however it reads, the meaning is the same: Your pastor deserves to be taken care of.

I am so thankful that even though Oasis Church began in a trailer after I forfeited a very good salary at my sending church (and a promise of much more if I stayed), they still found ways to compensate me and give raises before I mentioned anything. Over the years, our leaders, while dealing with very tight budgets and many challenges—like many churches experience—have consistently shown that they appreciate and care for me by giving me various blessings I did not ask for: the pastor's sabbatical, generous vacations, and raises when I did not think I needed or wanted them.

Several years ago, to show their love for me, one of our original founding members, who was once again serving in the council, asked them (without my knowledge) to compensate me at the level of pastors in other churches our size. This meant they would give me a very large raise over the following three years. I fought it when I found out, believing many others on our staff needed it and deserved raises as well.

Because the council decides on my compensation, I don't have a voice in it and never have or want to. But this time, I said, "No, I can't accept it." The leaders reminded me that if I died (not a pleasant thought) or left, they would have to pay the next pastor—a person who might be much younger and less experienced than I, the founding pastor—that salary. In the end, their perspective considered preparing the church for my demise. Ouch!

In all seriousness, what a gesture of appreciation and love. I was overwhelmed by it and still am. I told our business manager to wait and not give it to me the first year. I told them, "Others need it more; our ministry might need that first year's raise more than I do." He did as I asked. Then, I was called to a luncheon with this founding member, whom we all respect and love. He proceeded to call me on the carpet about what I had done. He reminded me that this was one area out of my hands, and the council had decided it, and I was not to change it. He then took it to the council. I agreed, and eventually, they even had our church vote to add this to our constitution, stipulating that no one, not even the pastor, can change his salary. Ha. (I might be one of very few pastors who got in trouble for not taking a raise.)

I can't imagine ever leaving this church, not that I had ever done so. But the love and the appreciation they showed through that gesture will last me the rest of my life. Imagine if your pastor felt that way. Well, he can. If you are in leadership who decides policy, you can do all kinds of things to honor and love him. It doesn't have to be with double-digit pay raises. Get creative. Just start with a sabbatical. Perhaps his family needs counseling, or possibly he does; or maybe there are other ways to show them your love.

When you send them on sabbatical, you can add some remuneration you saved up for, such as a special trip, cruise, counseling while they are gone, or even a gym membership. Ok, maybe that last one isn't a good proposition. But you get the idea. The NFL sends their Super Bowl star to Disney World. Maybe send yours somewhere since they are the quarterback of your team. They would not want to be called the MVP, but you get what I'm saying.

On the "*pay me now or pay me later*" argument, consider this: if you are worried about compensation, why wouldn't you spend on your current pastor (i.e., with the sabbatical), rather than pay a needed replacement? You may even end up needing to pay more for the replacement, and perhaps before they've earned it! A sabbatical policy will be an excellent example of the "pay me now" portion.

Be the Leader

Yes, be the one. Be the one who leads out on this. Don't wait on someone else, like the pastor or another leader. They may all be waiting, too. Don't let fear paralyze you. Don't let other fears keep you from it. I promise you the church will survive his being gone for a while. It's a win-win for you and the church.

Remember that church council member (Dennis) who brought the sabbatical policy up to the council? I will always be so thankful for him. He had been a pastor and had to leave the ministry over painful events. He understood firsthand the pressures and the needs of pastors and their families. He also explained the need to the church and did a video message to ensure everyone understood. He gave me and our church a gift I will never forget and will forever be grateful for.

He knew what I had been through, all the pressures, and he took the arrows and the questions and saved me so much from the heavy lifting. I hope there will be someone in your church who can do this for your pastor. Maybe that person is *you*. Will you step up?

Don't let fear paralyze you

Fear paralyzes. Churches are the worst at taking risks. We say we believe in living by faith, but we do little to show it when it means stepping out into the unknown and doing something we've never done before.

Yes, sabbaticals will likely be a new thought to most in your church.

Yes, there will possibly be some resistance.

Yes, it will cost you some funds and time.

And yes, it will be worth it.

A famous church saying goes, "We've never done it like that before." Nope, you haven't, and that is why you probably haven't continued to grow or why you keep having pastor turnover. The old saying is still true: The definition of insanity is doing the same thing over and over that did not work the first time and thinking it will work this time. The COVID-19 pandemic is over. We must do a lot of things differently. We are all out of our comfort zone.

After many years of sabbaticals (some as long as six months), other churches in our area now have sabbatical policies. I have yet to see a church suffer from its pastor's absence. In every case I know, these churches continued to grow and have only gotten stronger, and they have happier and healthier pastors.

Remember, sabbaticals are a biblically sound practice. Consider Hebrews 10, which reads, "Now the just shall live by faith" (Hebrews 10:38 KJV), and Hebrews 11, which reads, "Now faith is confidence in what we hope for and assurance about what we do not see" (Hebrews 11:1).

May more churches live out this truth!

8

Planning the Church Sabbatical Policy

There is no authoritative book on churches planning their sabbatical policy. There are several books available, and I will list a few at the end of the book you are reading; however, they are very subjective regarding the church and movement they are a part of. Most of what I have read on this topic is very scant. In this chapter, I share some ideas about how we prepared our policy along with other tools, but in the end, it is up to you and your church to map your way. These are just several ideas to get you started:

1. **Deciding among the leaders who will make decisions on having sabbaticals.**

I believe this is the most significant step. Depending on your church's structure, it may take several meetings for all to come together.

2. **Determining who will be able to take sabbaticals.**

It can be only the senior and lead pastor initially, or another executive or senior team member. If you are the sole pastor, then that is an easy step. I would not suggest starting too big and incorporating all staff at the start. You will need some experience first. Let the leaders who take the first sabbaticals come back with a follow-up on what they learned, what they did right, and what would need to be stopped or improved as to your sabbatical policy.

3. **When implementing sabbaticals, planning can help you prevent problems before they happen.**

One way to achieve this is to ensure that your sabbatical policy and the staff vacation and leave policies work well together. You can't have too many people out at once, and that includes considering not only sabbaticals but vacations. Non-pastoral staff need to be able to get breaks, too, even if they don't get to enjoy the gift of a sabbatical. I can't emphasize enough how important it is to plan ahead. This can help you avoid last-minute decisions and smooth out details with enough time.

4. **Timing needs to be considered.**

We have had pastors take their sabbaticals at various times, but most often, it is around spring, after Easter, or during summer. However, the times you choose will be based on your team, the church calendar, and holidays. For instance, we have a huge Christmas light display that draws up to 50,000 people from our community each year during the entire month of December. It would not be wise to send the director of the largest, month-long outreach of the year on sabbatical during Christmas time. We would not even consider any staff person being gone during this season because it is "all-hands-on-deck" for all staff and volunteers during December.

5. Determining how long someone must be full-time with the church before they get a sabbatical and how long their sabbatical should be.

To qualify for a sabbatical, we require being at the church as a full-time pastor or executive team member for at least five years, and then every five years afterward. The sabbatical starts at two months after five years of service, then increases to three months at ten years, four at fifteen, five at twenty, and six months at twenty-five years. I am the only one on our team who qualifies for the six months' time away. (After twenty-five years and six months, you either retire, they retire you, or you die, but no more than six months.) That is just with us, though. You come up with your own guidelines. Biblically, the ground was on sabbatical after six years, and in the seventh year, it rested, and so did the farmer. I don't think God is legalistic in that regard, but it is fine if someone wants to do it that way. We found tracking and planning for sabbatical leaves in five-year increments is easier. We are sharing our Oasis Sabbatical Policy, along with a few other examples, at the back of this book for your review.

6. Establishing a plan for the Sabbatarian.

(Yes, it is a real word[26]. It means someone who adheres to the sabbath.)

Each such plan will vary from person to person. It can be a form that the person fills out, stating their goals for their sabbatical. You can also find a few examples at the back of this book.

The staff and council will need to plan how they will cover the role and responsibilities while their pastor is away (the who, what, and where). Other staff and lay volunteers can do this. The person leaving and the leaders need to plan with plenty of time to avoid as many ball-drops as possible. There is no perfect scenario, just as there is no perfect church or even a perfect Sunday.

Details of the person's plans while away are essential, but they should also include phone numbers, emergency contact information, and the names of individuals who can reach the pastor if needed. It is essential to remember that the person on sabbatical leave needs to be able to unplug, so church members and staff should be reminded to refrain from contacting them. The church, their ministry, and any crisis that comes up while the person is on sabbatical leave can be handled by someone else. Just a reminder: we will all be gone someday, whether by moving away or by moving on up, so plan as if they are gone for good. This will help all involved take their roles, the needed time, and their talents very seriously.

Of course, there are times when contacting the person on sabbatical leave might be necessary, such as the death or sudden serious illness of a loved one or someone close to them. We inform our church that if you believe you need to reach out to the one gone, to run it by the Senior Pastor or his designated person—no one else can make the decision. That is the only way to give each person true time away to unwind and recharge.

At Oasis, we have even removed the person on leave from all our staff and church emails (and that also goes for me). This is a scary thing for the Sabbatarian as well as the church staff and family, but it's helpful.

You get the most overwhelming feeling of dreadful anticipation when you have taken long, extended leaves and return to thousands of emails. I have seen some executives and pastors give a specific person access to their church account so they can answer and cull out the emails that someone else can do before the pastor's return. Someone else can probably answer or delete 90 percent of them; for the important ones, answer them with the directions of the person who is taking the sabbatical.

7. Deciding how you will pay for them (or not).

Obviously, I feel the person should be paid while away. Not only that, but you should have a policy of how they will repay the church if they leave upon returning. You can turn to the appendix for our sample policies and what we ask upon returning. The church must be protected from a minister taking extended leave only to come back, resign, and go elsewhere. I haven't heard of this, but I would suggest you create an agreement on this subject.

8. Making a written agreement.

Co-write a contract or agreement with the person taking the sabbatical leave. This agreement should be signed and dated by the recipient of the sabbatical and the church leader overseeing the sabbatical policies. This way, there is no room for misunderstanding. If something that needs to be changed or agreed upon is unique to that person, then that can be added.

I would be careful not to detail too much about what they need to do, how, and the timing of it. You want them to unplug and not worry about too many details or how to please those they are responsible for. For example, I do not ask our pastors to read a certain number of books, attend a certain number of church services, or keep a detailed account of everything they do. I feel this takes away the joy and freedom of the sabbatical. I believe asking for a plan from them is a good idea to make them think, pray, and plan through this time away. The worst thing would be to wing it. It might be good for a day or even a week, but not for a month or three months, much less six months. A discussion—before the dates' approval—to go over their plans with those overseeing the policy is fitting, in case there are things someone might miss or that the leadership (without dictating everything) feels might be helpful to them.

It is appropriate to have some minimal expectations from the leadership that would truly enhance the sabbatical for the pastor and his church.

9. Drawing up clear instructions on what is expected after they return.

During the planning stages—before the pastor goes on sabbatical—agree on how he will share upon returning what he did and may have learned during his time away. This can be a paper or an email. There are no wrong or right answers; this will not be a test. It is worthwhile to ask for some accountability, even if it is: "I went to the mountains and fished for ten days and then to the beach and sat on the sand for eight." I could not do that, but some can.

10. Considering the learning curve.

As with anything, they say, practice makes perfect. Therefore, consider the learning curve for the church leadership and the Sabbatarian when rejoining the staff and day-to-day ministry. It is easy to miss, but striking a delicate balance is crucial. Coming back refreshed, renewed, restored, energetic, and with your creative juices flowing, only to be met with hesitancy, obstacles, daily issues, and a staff that has not experienced a sabbatical, requires prayer on everyone's part. After four sabbaticals, I have learned it is harder than it seems. There are awkward moments, and it takes time to re-integrate into the rat race we call ministry. If you are a lead pastor, be cautious not to come back and dump all your new visions, plans, and dreams in the first meeting. I know it is hard. I come back with pages of ideas and plans. Not that I try to. But it begins to flow after three to six weeks off, and I have a pen and pad nearby. So, please don't share it all in the first week you are back; you will scare your team off and then need another sabbatical. It's a standing joke at the Oasis campus that when I'd return from a cross-country bike ride or an extended sabbatical, time alone for days frees my mind to dream and think *way* too much. Ha! Again, a re-entry plan is as important as a plan for leaving and going away.

11. Keeping in mind that establishing and planning sabbaticals takes time..

Others and I who have taken sabbaticals recommend at least a year out to schedule the sabbatical. *Get it on the calendar* and ensure there are as few conflicts as possible. Six months before the sabbatical is expected to happen, the person planning their leave should submit their plan and goals. This is submitted to the appropriate team, which will review and approve it. It may seem like a long time (in some churches, it may be shorter, while in others, it may take longer). It is easy for it to slip up on us, and then the planning is not in place to ensure a healthy, fun, and productive sabbatical, whether for the person going or the ones taking on the mantle while the Sabbatarian is away. If you are fortunate enough to have a staff, I suggest not putting all the responsibility on them. Share it with lay leadership; they will be more than happy to support the person going. It also builds their leadership and helps them grow into stronger leaders. This is a huge benefit for the church, as it can help identify new leaders and further equip the ones we already have. Most of us are afraid to ask and be told "no." Do it anyway. It is not on us if someone says no; it is between them and God. Don't take it personally.

Having a plan well in advance not only helps you stay on track and build new leaders, but it also allows the person taking the sabbatical to dream and get excited, which keeps them motivated to work hard, knowing there's light and rest at the end of the tunnel.

I have never shared this with anyone, but for almost twenty years, I have started dreaming and planning for my next sabbatical as soon as I return from the current one. I went to the church calendar once and put my sabbatical on it four years in advance. Of course, no one looks that far ahead, but it is funny when someone eventually finds it. Now, *that* is what I call planning! I can't tell you how exciting it is to know you have an extended time just for you, God, and your family.

It saddens me to think that so many pastors never get this chance; they go through their whole ministry tired, discouraged, and ultimately disappointed in themselves and what they have accomplished in their lives and ministry. On a sabbatical, we have time to have God speak to us, convict us, plant new visions and dreams, and give us a whole new burst of energy for the ministry ahead. It is miraculous. It is *biblical*.

9

Planning the Sabbatical

Now that the leadership team has laid out a policy (put in writing and gone through the procedure your church requires), the ball is in the Sabbatarian's court.

It is time to plan and prepare.

A word of caution to you: before getting too far down the road of planning, ensure your ministry is healthy enough for you to be gone for any length of time. Sadly, I have had to say "no" to people on our team about a sabbatical, even though they had been at Oasis long enough to earn it. There are no absolutes when getting a sabbatical. Yes, you earn it, but in the end, it's a gift from the church, and the greatest appreciation of that gift is to prepare your ministry for your absence. This seems to go without saying, but it is easy for someone to be blinded to their shortcomings in preparation. So . . . before you get to the many fun parts of planning, make sure you prepare your teams and ministries. We will not allow a sabbatical until our leadership knows that the person leaving has readied their teams, leaders, and volunteers to cover their absence. They must have a fully staffed and trained team of volunteers with the necessary systems in place to ensure their day-to-day responsibilities run smoothly. If your ministry is poorly staffed or organized while you are present, how will it work when you are gone?

Every church leader, whether pastor or team member, equips the saints. Ephesians 4:11-12 is very clear about this. If you are a leader, equipping should begin long before your planned sabbatical. However, if you are just a manager and not a leader, then I question whether you should need or take the leader's sabbatical. I know this may sound harsh, but I am so passionate about sabbaticals that I want the church to be blessed by them. Not dreading them and wishing we did not have them (or worse, to have such a bad experience that the leadership kills the sabbatical ministry for pastors and leaders altogether).

So, my loving word to the potential Sabbatarian: do your work *now*, and when you request a sabbatical, you'll be doing your ministry so well that the leaders (lay or staff) will be excited to send you off for a well-deserved time of renewal and restoration.

Now, assuming your teams are healthy and prepared, church leadership has approved your sabbatical, and the dates are set . . . *What now?*

This is the fun part.

Sit down, pray, and think about how long you'd be away, what you would do, and so on. You probably already know some of those answers if you've had some time off.

Create a bucket list (if you don't already have one). What have you dreamt of doing someday? What would you do if money were no object? (We will talk about money in the next chapter.) It may not happen today, right now, but you can start dreaming. You are praying for God to lead the way, right? God might work it out.

What if you are married? Discuss your bucket list with your spouse after you've dreamed and created your list. Ask about their ideas and thoughts. Get their thumbs-up or down on them. Don't get defensive if they think some of your ideas are dumb or unrealistic. Just listen. Then, discuss it some more. You can agree to disagree; they aren't the last word necessarily, but they love you more than anyone. So, yes, *listen*.

Make time as a family to do some fun things you can't do in a week during vacation. Consider what is on *their* bucket lists. Again, someone with grown kids has a different reality of what they may do. With kids still at home, they need to be considered, but *not* allowed to decide your entire sabbatical.

If possible, I would also caution you about spending the entire time away with your family. There is something about getting alone with God and listening to Him. Also, it would be best if you had some time for yourself. This sounds so selfish, but it's actually the opposite. It reminds us to care for and love our families; however, you need time to recharge and be refreshed to be all they need you to be. I can tell you from experience that camping for weeks with little ones, taking a cross-country trip with the family or the grandkids is great and can be a lot of fun, but you also need a chance to recoup after time together.

Do your part to plan and prepare, commit your work to the Lord, and your plans will be established (Proverbs 16:3). Nothing is better than having God bless your rest.

Final Thoughts

How can we afford for our pastor to take a sabbatical?

This is the last and one of the most important questions we want to address. It must be prayed over and planned out. It is possible. It is a necessity. It is like a family pondering whether they could ever afford a child. Most people would never have children if resources stood in their way. As it happens, when you have children—if it is important and a priority—you make it work. You find a way because it matters.

I'd say you have no choice.

If you can't afford to give your pastor a sabbatical, plan to spend that much or more searching for your next pastor. Along with time and resources come a lot of risk and uncertainty, and guess what? . . . He may ask for a sabbatical anyway. The way I see it, ignoring the need to be prepared is not an option.

Just as the land needs rest or it will be depleted and become sterile for future crops, your pastor, his family, and your church need rest. As mentioned in earlier chapters, practical ways exist to begin and implement the process. Remember, this is just the tip of the iceberg. Every church and every pastor's situation is different. But if you see the value of having a sabbatical policy and recognize you do not have another option but to do it, you will find a way to make it happen. The following are some ideas that may help you in your decision-making and planning process so the pastor and the church can afford his next sabbatical:

- **Budget a few years ahead** with a little set aside each month.

- **Take a special offering** for your pastor's sabbatical, maybe even a mini-campaign. (What capital campaign is more important than building and renewing your shepherd, leader, servant, and God's called man to your church?)

- **Ask other leaders** to help fund or pay for guest speakers while your pastor is gone.

- **Invite deacons or church lay leaders** who can speak and fill the pulpit. Don't even start on, "Well . . . they are not as good as the pastor." They may not have the same gifts or experience, but your people will give them a lot of grace, knowing they are allowing the pastor time away. You might even find some future speakers when your church transitions from one pastor to another. Why? Because the reality is, someday you will have to, whether by his being called elsewhere or by death, burnout, or other reasons.

(The former would be sooner than later if you don't give him a sabbatical.)

- **Talk to retired pastors** who can come in and fill the pulpit, maybe even do some volunteer work. They will work and serve for little to nothing (or nothing at all if they have prepared well for retirement). I hope not to call it *retirement* someday, since I don't believe God has given that word to pastors. Of course, I won't be able to lead at the level I have been at for several decades now. I understand that someday I will have to step back into less stressful and less busy roles, but just as meaningful. I hope and pray that Oasis and I have adequately prepared so I can afford to fill in for pastors who need sabbaticals. I would love to serve the church in this way as I slow down. There may be others who share this perspective.

- **Consider local pastors and their staff** who can also come to fill in. Then, you can reciprocate for them when they take their sabbatical. Our church has had a teaching team for over twenty years. We have allowed our various lay and full-time pastors to periodically fill the pulpit for churches that may need a guest speaker. We are part of His kingdom ministry, and taking time away is a way to teach your church to be kingdom-minded and recall that we are one church—*His church.*

- **Engage missionaries** who come home from the field, either permanently or for a season, and love to share and serve other churches.

- **You can tap on another staff member** to help with the administrative duties. Many laypeople can help in this area—whether they believe they can, or you believe it for them. I have learned this truth through my sabbaticals. You won't know till you try it. Your church—His church—will survive you not being there. That day will come, so begin preparing now.

- **Check organization**s like Lilly Endowment, Inc., which have sabbatical programs and grants for pastors. (They have strict guidelines regarding tenures, education levels, and so on, which will be good to get familiar with.) For instance, although I have almost fifty years of full-time ministry experience, I do not qualify because I have never finished my master's degree. But some of you can have a full ride paid for by Lilly. You can find out all about it online.[27]

Lodging can be another big expense that seems out of touch with the average pastor or church. However, with some planning and research, you can learn about organizations such as Focus on the Family,[28] which also has a pastor hospitality ministry. They list several places that give pastors free (or almost free) lodging. Our church has a nine-bedroom, nine-bathroom, 100-year-old beachside home that was once a bed and breakfast, which our people purchased to house pastors and missionaries for short stays. The Oasis Beach House's[29] maximum stay is seven days once a year. But if you put together two to five locations for your sabbatical, you might be able to stay in nice places for little to no cost. Our rates for standard guests online through *Vrbo* range from $125 to $399 a night during the winter in Hollywood Beach, Florida, but a pastor stays for $15 to $25 a night, which doesn't even pay maintenance costs. Why do we charge anything? To make sure you have skin in the game. We have a large mortgage, and it costs a lot to maintain this property on the beach. If someone books, we want them to show up. The "snowbirds," as we call them (people from Canada), pay our mortgage, and our pastors and missionaries get to stay at a beautiful historical home with an incredible location, pool, and deck just seventy-five feet from the Atlantic Ocean.

The Billy Graham's home called Billy's Home Place,[30] where Tonia and I had the privilege of staying, also has a pretty good list of places to stay for little or no cost to pastors. There are conference centers, as well as other religious locations, that offer housing for pastors on sabbaticals at little to no expense. Spend some time online, and you will find many of these items on your list to check out.

There are always friends and family if they have an extra apartment, home, or vacation place where you can stay for a little while. Don't be afraid to ask or let your lay leadership reach out and ask. There are people in your church you can count on, and your leaders can ask those who have places to go. There is so much more out there than you might expect, but it will take some planning and checking. Go for it.

- For those who love the great outdoors, "borrow, beg, or steal" (okay, don't steal, it was just an expression, ha!) a tent or camper and head to the mountains, desert, or woods.

- If you must travel a long distance, you can reach out to friends and members who might work for an airline and see if they would allow you to use one of their companion passes.

These are just some ways *every church* can send their pastor on sabbatical, and many times, even afford it for little to no cost. It is fun to explore all the ways, maybe even form a team of church members who can help find these places. Pastor: Don't do it all yourself. Those around you love you and would love to help you with this. They are not just blessing you, but they are blessing your church by enabling you to be away and cut back on your budget and the church's.

Ok, you've convinced us! Where do we go from here?

No one can tell you how to develop, prepare, or create a sabbatical policy. However, I hope this book will provide you with some ideas to get started, but keep in mind there is no one-size-fits-all. I have also included in the book's appendix several examples from a few churches of pastors I know, who have allowed us to share some of their documents, including their sabbatical policies. They will be helpful to you as you develop your own. I know I'm not good at creating from scratch, so when I see ideas from someone else, it sparks more of my own, and off I go. Hopefully, this will also help you.

Condensed Summary

In earlier chapters, we have shared the following major points in more detail, where we expanded on how our policy and model evolved.

Highlighting the Essentials

- **Pray.** We will assume every stage from start to finish will be covered in prayer; therefore, we will not mention it constantly. But do not discount how God can do so much more than we can if we ask. Pray alone, with your spouse if you have one, and with leaders around you.

- **Share.** Involve your leadership team, who is empowered to make decisions on behalf of your church. If you don't have a formal team, build one for this endeavor to ensure that it is not just the pastor deciding to take a sabbatical. People with credibility will make a huge impact. I owe Dennis DaCosta a huge debt of gratitude for being the face and frontman to establish a pastoral sabbatical policy in our church. As a former pastor and leader, Dennis had first-hand knowledge of our need for biblical rest and respect for our church.

- **Find.** Take time to locate the right books, articles, or other materials to share with your leaders. Our plan, for as long as we can afford to, is to give this book free of charge to any church or pastor who wants one. That is one of the primary objectives of our Love

Cities, Love Pastors church-wide campaign. We will make it available at the best possible price for teams considering a sabbatical policy. We will *never* make a cent on a book. Our call is to bless other pastors and churches. This is why we are also offering it online as an eBook. You can also find it on Amazon, Barnes & Noble, and similar sites.

- **Explore.** Spend some time discussing what you read. Talk about concerns, fears, and apprehensions. Hopefully, there is one in the group who is so excited that they will ignite those who are not early adopters and pioneers. Remember, not everyone will get it. Don't let one nay-sayer derail your future ministry, health, and the church's health. (There's always at least one.) Bring as many leaders as possible in that first group, but don't let one stop you. I hate to be so blunt, but I've had to tell our staff many times over the years that to move forward with our call, vision, and mission, it may mean there will be subtraction. Generally, *in ministry, you don't have multiplication without subtraction*. Do I hear "Amen"? Yes, you could lose someone (and sometimes more than one). If you feel God is leading you and it is needed, then be willing to lose some. Harsh—I know—but there was this man, one time, named Jesus . . . Okay, enough said.

- **Write.** Once the leadership team is on board, start writing your policies. It is not rocket science. As you will see from the ones I have provided, which are simple and to the point. Don't make them too detailed and complicated.

- **Incorporate.** Include budgets and how both the church and the pastor can underwrite them.

- **Measure.** Decide the length of the sabbatical and include how it increases with years—which I highly recommend. Reward those who serve for long tenures. They are to be honored with more time. This also encourages them to stay and others to come so they can partake in this valuable ministry.

- **Clarify.** Define who is eligible to take sabbaticals and other critical items. The sabbatical policy samples in the appendix of this book refer to this. They also include paying back the church for the cost of the sabbatical when leaving within a year of taking it, planning for the sabbatical, and recapping upon returning.

- **Vote.** Once you have all this written out, vote or decide, however your church does it, to enshrine as policy beyond this one time. This helps to eliminate doubt and division, or prevent future leadership from arbitrarily changing or discontinuing the sabbatical. If it needs to be voted on by the church, this is worth considering early on, after much education on the topic, sermons, and leaders sharing their support. It is also worth taking pulpit time for this. It is as biblical as any topic you can preach on. (As I've highlighted in previous chapters, our church doesn't vote on things like this; it is left to our church council of men and women, voted annually by our church. I love this.)

- **Begin.** Once the sabbatical policy is voted on, begin the planning process. It may take six months or up to two years, especially for the first time, so get started as soon as possible. Remember, if taking the sabbatical were to become an emergency in your life as a pastor, the stress and other negative issues that can arise when you plan in a hurry would only add to your burden.

- **Assign.** Commission volunteers to cover the various tasks that need to be done while you are away. You know your church, your missions, and other commitments better than anyone, so make a list. It will be daunting and scary, perhaps, but well worth it. (Sadly, I know only a few pastors who have taken sabbaticals. But I have never met anyone who regretted it, lost their church, or hurt the ministry because of it—not one. I am excited to see more young pastors interested in establishing the sabbatical policy early. Praise God. I'm so proud of them.)

- **Arrange** chronologically. Create a timeline of the various steps leading up to and throughout the sabbatical so that everyone is on the same page.

- **Focus.** Keep the goal in mind and how exciting this will be. Lining up all the speakers, tasks, and seemingly endless details does not have to be scary or debilitating. Remember, you are only one of a small percentage of pastors with such a loving and supportive church that allows you to do this. We prayerfully hope this percentage will grow with time.

- **Involve.** Make sure you include all your immediate family members in the planning. The family aspect can be the most challenging, especially if you still have small children at home. (My sabbaticals began when our boys were moving on to college, and only one was in high school, in his senior year.) Make sure your spouse is in on as much of your planning and preparation as they wish to be, and remember, they must be on board, feel included, and considered. I won't go into specifics, but there have been a few times, some big and small changes in my sabbaticals, out of respect for Tonia, her needs, and even her concerns during various seasons. *I can't overemphasize this point enough.* However, I don't think I have ever heard of a spouse who was not excited for their husband and what it would do for him and his ministry.

Now, I want to spend more time on this section than on other areas of planning, as it is probably the most important part of the process and yet has the most significant chance of being overlooked by the pastor and the church.

While I don't think the spouse should be able to veto everything, they should be highly involved and supportive. If they aren't, then you probably have other issues that need to be resolved before the sabbatical, and maybe only an outside counselor can help you address them.

This leads me to mention that some may seek counseling for various reasons during their sabbatical, when they can work on themselves, their family, marriage, and other issues without having to do so in town or while trying to work and lead a family. This one opportunity might become the greatest blessing for some pastors. (Details of counseling and such do not need to be put in writing to the board, in my opinion. These can be better categorized as 'general planning.')

Let me reiterate: a sabbatical is no vacation. Vacations should still be taken with the family; however, this doesn't mean the family cannot travel and spend some time with the pastor during his sabbatical—although, for the pastor to truly recharge, there must be time for him to decompress, spend time in prayer, read, breathe, and be alone. We have already covered how vacations can be, and while important, some can be more tiring than the ministry.

Time with family during the pastor's sabbatical should be included in the planning, from budgeting to logistics. But what about when he has gone, and there are family issues and needs to attend to? This is complicated. Each family must work this out and factor it in during planning. It was not that complicated for Tonia and me during our season, but we still had lots of details to work on, from lawn mowing (which I did) to cleaning the pool (which I also did) to paying bills, and so on. Every responsibility that has been my job throughout our marriage had to be worked out. (WARNING: Pastor, when you leave, having your wife oversee these items might backfire, and you'll come back to find out they hired someone else. I lost my lawn-cutting and pool-cleaning jobs. I liked doing them but as I aged and with my crazy schedule, I stank at them. In the end, I am glad she hired someone else, although I haven't told her. Maybe she won't be reading this book. But if she is . . . I love you, Babe!)

Pastors with small children or even young teens, you may need to rally up grandparents, in-laws (outlaws might even do sometimes, ha), church members, friends, and others who can step in and help. A few may even help with some chores. (Church leadership: Maybe you should consider spending money assisting the spouse with various things while the pastor is gone. What a great investment in the spouse's ministry and person. There are *so, so* many ways you can help.)

Pastor, you need to unplug from the church, including all church correspondence and interactions with church members. This needs to be formally stated and executed. However, even though it should go without saying, you should *not* unplug from your family. I believe that, if possible, you should communicate at least once a day to check in with your spouse and reconnect, unless you agree to stay longer for specific reasons. They should not feel abandoned; otherwise, your sabbatical won't be all God planned for you, nor will it be what you and the church envisioned.

Sabbaticals could be an opportunity to spend a little more time with your spouse and the children one-on-one, since vacations don't afford that.

If you must stay home for a part of the sabbatical, while it is not ideal and may complicate your plans, it is sometimes necessary. Plan accordingly to get away from the house. Consider doing things with your spouse during the day, or pick up the kids from school if you never do, so your spouse can get some rest and a break. It is your time. Use it any way you like. (Legally, of course, and within your church's values code. Robbing banks might seem exciting, but it might not be wise, ha!)

The topic of family alone could be a chapter, but it is challenging to provide definitive answers to the numerous complex situations within families. Remember, the church *is* a family. It is a community. If they can't lift loads and help your family more than ever during this time, then we are not being the church. This also allows some of your church family to be engaged in this exciting experience.

Lastly, I want to mention another item that may be overlooked. And that is how it enriches the church and the pastor when you celebrate the launch day and his return home. This conversation about the pastor's sabbatical and all the details that accompany it concerns the health of both the pastor and the church. And just like it is among family members, how wonderful it is when love permeates the relationship. Such is this opportunity to bless the pastor's comings and goings. Show him a lot of love every time.

Okay, let's finish off our *highlighting the essentials* list:

- **Celebrate.** I can attest, from personal experience, that leaving is traumatic and is harder than you or the pastor will ever publicly admit. It will be much more emotional than imagined. (It ripped my heart out the first time, along with being so scared of so many unknowns.) A great send-off could include a celebration service, maybe a dessert and coffee time, and more importantly, a time of dedication to the Lord for the pastor and those who are stepping up to fill the many roles during the sabbatical. A commitment to him and his family that you will pray for them and be there for any need that arises. This can make an already emotional parting a little easier and more reassuring. The first sendoff is the hardest; however, I must add that each time is still challenging.

- **Rejoice** together. Returning can also be a time of celebration, almost like the "prodigal son" has returned. What no one—except the pastor—will realize is that it is awkward for him. He has missed a lot of your special moments, grieving with families, loving, and leading both the paid and volunteer staff. I have felt like a fifth wheel coming back from a sabbatical and almost felt like a visitor. It is not because of anything anyone says or does, but it is me, my emotions, and my feelings. There is guilt in leaving and returning, that somehow you might be missing a milestone in someone's life, missing the funeral of a beloved member or friend, and not being around to pull your weight. After all, no one else gets a pastor's sabbatical but the pastor. There's guilt and all kinds of emotions going on. Give them some slack. Give them lots of hugs and reassurance that they were missed, but you are glad they got to experience a sabbatical. When you start, it is difficult to include these details unless you are with someone who has gone through his sabbaticals three or four times (but who's counting, right?).

What I can say about the experience of launching and coming back from my sabbaticals is that every return, to some extent, is the same. These emotions do not seem to lessen with each subsequent sabbatical; on the contrary, they remain a part of the experience, but they are also informed and mitigated by every loving gesture from those around me. I am grateful every time.

Conclusion

Before we part, let's revisit what we have covered together: how sabbaticals came about as part of our Oasis Church policy for us. I have shared my story as a young pastor with a new planter church, addressing many questions and reasons for resistance and hesitancy, and touching on the biblical context (remember, not theology) of our sabbatical policy. We touched on the role of the pastor, expectations and pressures, and hurricane-type challenges that could've thwarted my ministry and left me out of it altogether—had it not been for a previous implementation of our sabbatical policy. We journeyed together through the possible goals, vision, and emotions that may go into planning and executing your sabbatical. We mentioned the difference between vacation and sabbatical, which may help you articulate your need for both. We visited the unsuspecting and unintended push towards burnout that some of us received as part of our seminary training back in the day, when I was a pupil. We laid out an outline for planning, dreaming, budgeting, and considering family and those around you. All these come to you from decades of ministry experience.

We have also addressed the church leaders and those who can make a difference for the pastor. We talked about the cost of giving him a sabbatical, the price that comes from not investing in the pastor's physical and spiritual well-being, and how this is an investment that ultimately affects the church directly. We covered the who, the why, and how long of a sabbatical as we do it at Oasis; what to do and what not to do when the pastor is away, and how beneficial it is to put it all in writing for this year and for years to come.

Yes, there are no absolutes in getting a sabbatical, but a template of what is expected and helpful can be built upon over time, year after year.

You have read my story, the Oasis story. You can find in these pages stories of others who also sought to exchange the load with a lighter one in Christ. Now, it is time for you to write yours. I hope this book has stirred you and your congregation into actionable love. A love for the pastor and a love for the congregation, because we are better when we love each other well, invest in one another, and spur each other to obedience into the abundant life that Christ leads us to. The life traced by His parameters and rhythms found in this book we treasure—the Bible—especially in this world and the generation God chose for us to serve.

I also have high hopes when I see the younger generations serving with their all, their lives surrendered to the call of Christ to feed His sheep, sharing bountifully their gifts and talents to serve His church. Twenty, thirty, forty, fifty-somethings in the trenches of ministry twenty-four seven with little to no respite.

CONCLUSION

Every one of these pastors and their families lies heavy on my heart and has inspired this project in your hands. May the call to serve the Lord and His church be as clear as ever. May other leaders and the church rally around the pastor to birth new and healthy biblical rhythms to accomplish every good work that our Savior God prepared in advance for us to do before the beginning of time.

The Lord your God wants you to succeed in ministry, and so do I.

Suddenly an angel shook him awake and said, "Get up and eat!"

He looked around and, to his surprise, right by his head were a loaf of bread baked on some coals and a jug of water. He ate the meal and went back to sleep.

The angel of God came back, shook him awake again, and said, "Get up and eat some more—you've got a long journey ahead of you."

He got up, ate and drank his fill, and set out. Nourished by that meal, he walked forty days and nights, all the way to the mountain of God, to Horeb. When he got there, he crawled into a cave and went to sleep.

Then the word of God came to him: "So Elijah, what are you doing here?"

(1 Kings 19:5-9 MSG))

Appendix

Sabbatical Policy Document Samples

Oasis Sabbatical Leave Policy

Sabbatical Leave

A sabbatical leave may be granted to full-time, pastoral staff who have served a minimum of 5 years. Sabbatical leave is subject to advance approval by the Senior Pastor. In most instances, only one pastor will be allowed to take a sabbatical leave at a given time.

After 5 years of service – 2 months plus vacation.
After 10 years of service – 3 months plus vacation.
After 15 years of service – 4 months plus vacation
After 20 years of service - 5 months plus vacation (CLARIFY minutes omit this number)
After 25 years of service – 6 months plus vacation

Pay will continue at the regular rate for employees on sabbatical leave. Vacation will continue to accrue, but paid holidays during the sabbatical can not be taken upon return. Years of Service include only years as a full-time pastor at Oasis Church unless the Senior Pastor makes an exception.

The following conditions must be met for a sabbatical to be granted:

1. The dates of the sabbatical leave must be submitted at least 6 months in advance and approved by the Senior Pastor
2. A plan must be submitted to the Senior Pastor to cover his ministry responsibilities during his absence.
3. A written proposal containing goals for the sabbatical including books to read, courses to take, travel, and other projects.
4. A signed agreement that he fully intends to return to full-time service at Oasis Church for a period of at least 1 year.

Within thirty (30) days of his return the pastor must submit a detailed, written report of what his activities and accomplishments during the sabbatical leave.

A pastor who takes a sabbatical must complete a year of service upon his return. If he does not, he will not be eligible for any separation pay and he will be asked to return the pay given him by the church during his sabbatical.

Sabbatical leave is granted. It does not accrue. It is not a vacation. It is an extended leave for personal and spiritual renewal. Once a sabbatical is taken, the employee is not eligible for another sabbatical for 5 years unless the Senior Pastor, in consultation with the Church Council, makes an exception.

WORK HARD. PLAY HARD.

Sabbatical Policy
City Rev Church

Purpose

City Rev Church Sabbatical Policy is in place for all full time pastors and directors on staff. The Sabbatical is to provide for physical, spiritual, and relational renewal and refreshment to help insure a healthy ministry staff. City Rev Church philosophy is to be able to lead at our highest capacity from a place of spiritual health.

Eligibility

Sabbatical leave is granted to full time pastors and directors after the completion of five full years of full time ministry and every fifth year thereafter.

Length of Time

The length of time for sabbatical leave is as follows:

- Full Time Pastors and Directors
    - Six weeks after 5 years of full time ministry
    - The length of sabbatical leave will increase by two weeks for every subsequent 5 years of service. (ie. 6 weeks after 5 years, 8 weeks after 10 years, 10 weeks after 15 years, etc.)

- Vision Team
    - Eight weeks after 5 years of full time ministry
    - The length of sabbatical leave will increase by two weeks for every subsequent 5 years of service. (ie. 8 weeks after 5 years, 10 weeks after 10 years, 12 weeks after 15 years, etc.)

Leave Time Details

Sabbatical leave is fully paid and is not intended to replace vacation time. The individual would be expected to take their vacation time in addition to the sabbatical leave. If the individual leaves within a year after returning from sabbatical leave, they must pay back the salary they were compensated during their leave time.

APPENDIX

Goal

The goal of the sabbatical is for physical, spiritual, and relational renewal. We believe that a key component to our health is to keep family first. With that in mind, our sabbaticals are also an investment in the family of the staff person. So a sabbatical should include activities that would enrich the staff member's spouse and family. It would also include a time set aside for spiritual growth. The hope is that a sabbatical would include rest, relaxation, and exercise.

Procedure

Submit a plan for sabbatical that would include dates and a plan that would detail the steps that would accomplish the purpose. Plans should be submitted 6 months prior to the start of sabbatical leave. (Please the Sabbatical Worksheet in the business templates)

Timing

The timing of the sabbatical leave should be at a time that would least likely affect the operation of the church and ministry. The summer months are the most likely choice.

Ministry Coverage

The sabbatical plan should include a plan for how the normal ministry duties will be covered. Those could be via several other staff and/or volunteers.

Return

There will be a plan for the pastor/director to ease back into the ministry position. In addition, a report that summarizes their leave, should be submitted to the direct report.

WORK HARD. PLAY HARD.

Sabbatical Worksheet

Ministry Leader:

Ministries:

Dates:

Section 1: Sabbatical Plan

1) What are your goals for your Sabbatical?

2) Who will be your contact person?

3) What is your strategy for disconnecting?

4) What will be your go-to source if you need a listening ear, counseling, etc.?

5) What is the basic itinerary for your trip?

6) What is your plan for re-entry?

7) What are the ways we can be praying for you?

APPENDIX

Section 2: Ministries in Your Absence

1) How are you planning to communicate with your teams about your sabbatical?

2) Please list who is covering your responsibilities.

3) What key events happen in your absence?

Pastor Kevin's Original Sabbatical Leave Request

Before a formal policy was adopted, Pastor Kevin had begun (but did not complete) an essay on sabbaticals. He intended to share it with the church elders to form a permanent policy. This here is the introduction to that essay. (And immediately, in the following pages, you will also find the sabbatical policy in Kevin's church, his sabbatical proposal, and the review upon his return.)

> After twenty-six years of ministry I've realized how easy it is to allow ministry to dictate my rhythm. There have been times I have guilted myself into believing this. After all, it's my calling. Ultimately, for whatever reason, unhealthy rhythms are just unhealthy. Archibald Hart says: "Humans were designed for camel travel, but most people are now acting like supersonic jets. In a nutshell, most of us are living too fast a pace . . .. The pace of modern life is stretching all of us beyond our limits. And we are paying for this abuse in the hand of painful currency of stress and anxiety."
>
> I would add, the cost is more painful than that. We are ultimately missing our truest calling; to love God and others. That means all the time, wherever we are. Most of the time that calling requires us to act in the ordinary, everyday routine of life.
>
> Julie Canlis, in her book, *Theology of the Ordinary*, says: "If you've ever heard it said that if you want to get something done, go ask a busy person. Know

that the same holds true for evangelicals! Essential to the evangelical nature is activism, particularly if it is the opportunity to do something great for God." Have we lost the importance of the ordinary over the desire for extraordinary? The drive to accomplish the latter causes us to rush past the former. However, it is the ordinary where real growth happens. The everyday rhythm of life is where the greatest level of intimacy with God is cultivated. It's where we most rely on the faith community around us. I would go as far as to say it is the ordinary that leads us to the extraordinary.

It would seem that Jesus was constantly surrounded by thousands of seekers who wanted the extraordinary. It would also seem that Jesus constantly delivered. Unfortunately, I've come to recognize that this is the very lens through which I prefer to see Jesus's ministry; the same reason the crowds followed him. The extraordinary is exciting. It is sensational, even mystical. As I read through Luke one more time I was struck by the rhythm and pace of Jesus. It was mostly in the ordinary three-mile-an-hour pace that Jesus taught his disciples. I picture myself as one of the twelve disciples saying, "Okay Jesus, aren't we done here? Can we move on now? Let's get to the next big thing." I believe Jesus's response would be, "Kevin, why are you in such a Hurry? Sit down, I have more for you here."

During my sabbatical Jesus challenged me to move at his pace. In fact, a big part of his message to me was: slow down, be quiet, pay attention and listen. I was challenged by Jesus to begin to evaluate my rhythm. I needed to discover what a sustainable rhythm looked like. Joe Walters, president of Soul Care Institute, proposed I seek the answer to this question "What are the "brines" I need to sit in to experience the transforming work of God?" For me the brines were essentials like: scripture, prayer, silence and solitude, and providential relationships. But not in the sense I had gone about them before. No longer was I to prescribe or dictate how God would speak to me. Gone are the days of my typical quiet time where I give God a few minutes to drop an extraordinary word on me for my daily meditation. Instead, I was being called to find real silence and solitude regularly so that God had my full attention to lead me to life transformation. Prayer looks different now. No more one way talks but a conversation that breaks through the surface and penetrates my soul. Time constraints don't work here. The sabbath discipline is more about being still and waiting than doing something on my spiritual checklist.

LSCC Sabbatical POLICY

LSCC recognizes the importance of our ordained pastoral and licensed ministerial staff. In our commitment to the growth, development and renewal for ministry of our ordained pastors and licensed ministers, LSCC shall administer a sabbatical leave program to be applied to all full-time ordained pastoral and licensed ministerial staff members.

Sabbatical leave is a carefully planned period of time in which an ordained pastor or licensed minister is granted leave away from his or her normal ministerial responsibilities in order to spend an extended period of time in study, reflection and renewal. Sabbatical leave is not a vacation, nor is it *only* continuing education.

Full-time Pastors and Ministry Staff may apply for sabbatical leave after completion of five years continuous service at LSCC. He or she will be eligible for another sabbatical leave after every five years of continuous service dated from the end of the previous sabbatical period. The following conditions and requirements will apply to all sabbaticals:

- The sabbatical period will be four to six weeks in length for Pastoral staff and six to eight weeks in length for the Lead Pastor.

- Full salary and benefits will be paid during the leave.

- Each ordained pastor or licensed minister will receive funds for travel and related expense (amount to be approved by the Lead Team)

- A summary report should be submitted to the Lead Team no later than thirty days after returning from the sabbatical.

- The sabbatical may not be used in looking for another job; and the pastor/staff must agree to remain with the church for at least one full year after the sabbatical. Should he/she leave for other than emergency or special situations, he will be required to repay the church for the sabbatical time.

APPENDIX

LSCC Application and Approval Process

The ordained pastor or licensed minister desiring the sabbatical shall fill out a written application that includes the following:

- Dates of the leave
- Reasons for the leave
- Potential benefits to the individual and the congregation
- A plan for covering job responsibilities during the leave
- What is to be accomplished by the leave – goals and objectives?
- A summary of anticipated expenses related to the leave
- The application must be approved by the Elders and Lead Team
- The written application should be submitted at least three months prior to the requested leave period for final approval.

At the end of the sabbatical leave the ordained pastor or licensed minister shall resume his or her normal duties.

WORK HARD. PLAY HARD.

Pastor Kevin's Sabbatical Proposal

Sabbatical Proposal for
Kevin Hartman
Submitted March 22, 2018

Purpose: Refinement in personal and professional relationship and leadership

This year, I have chosen the word "refine" to describe what I believe God is doing in me.
Refine = Remove impurities or unwanted elements from

PERSONALLY

God is challenging me to evaluate my approach to my relationship with Pam in the same way Jesus relates to his church. Since she was a little girl, Pam aspired to be a wife and mother. God gave Pam to me, in part, to fulfill her life-long ambitions. It is time to ask: what in me is hindering her from living out her God-given ambitions? I need His refinement.
Parenting adult children has been my life's greatest challenge. Navigating the needs of my 22 year-old, live at home daughter, my married 20 year-old daughter, my soon to be senior in high school 17 year-old daughter, while parenting a 6 year-old is a greater challenge than expected. Each need something unique from me. I want to refine my focus on what each needs at this stage in her life and give that to her.

PROFESSIONALLY

The last 18 months have been a stretch for me. Supervising up to 11 people at times is demanding. I've felt extremely inadequate. I've felt extremely fulfilled. I'm doing what I love. But the grind of putting together vision and strategy for the future of our ministry to families in Lee's Summit, is making me feel a bit stagnant. I'm ready to go! I want to be done with the planning and move to the execution. I am ready to see a new culture begin to emerge. I find myself wanting to fast-forward. I need to refine my thoughts and see what is distracting me from the focus needed to finish this process well.

Breakdown of Time

Beginning: May 21
Ending: June 24
Duration: 5 weeks

May 21-31: Relax
I am currently finalizing plans to travel to Daphne, Al, to spend time with Pam, the girls, and her parents for relaxation and refreshment. Her parents have a few small projects to complete (a relaxing and enjoyable thing for me) and the beach is nearby.

June 1-11: Prepare
As a precursor to week 4, I will spend this week reading and reflecting on the current status of my personal and professional health. I have a few books I would like to complete and anticipate some reading requirements to fulfill before going to Potters Inn.

June 12-16: Receive
I am currently finalizing plans to spend four days at Potters Inn participating in the Soul Care program. I look forward to times of refinement through one-on-one counsel and ministry from the Spirit. I will probably hit a few mountain bike trials while I'm there as well!

June 17-24: Reflect
This week will be structured in a way to give time to reflect on what I've learned. I anticipate times of setting personal and professional goals, connecting with people who have meant a great deal to me in my personal journey, and finalizing a report for our elders.

APPENDIX

Pastor Kevin's Review

Sabbatical Review
Kevin Hartman

June 24, 2018

Major themes:

Enjoy the Moment
I've watched every episode of Fixer Upper; you know, Chip and Joanna Gaines, Magnolia Farm, the people who flip houses. Chip is the risk taker. Joanna is the planner. Chip's favorite part of flipping a house is demo day; the day of the project he gets to break and destroy things. Joanna's favorite day of the project is putting the finishing touches on the house. It's easy to simply think, "Oh, they make a great team. One balances out the other." But, opposites cause friction. Friction causes heat. Early on in their relationship the friction caused problems. Over time they have learned a few key principles: appreciate the other's strengths, every step is necessary, and enjoy the moment. I realize reality TV isn't always reality. But, there is something about Chip and Joanna that seems real when I watch their show or read their books. They have learned to enjoy every moment of the journey. This reminder came early in my sabbatical and opened the door to more important things to which God was leading me.

Slow Down!
I must slow down in order to enjoy every moment of the journey. I wrote this in my sabbatical proposal: "The grind of putting together vision and strategy for the future of our ministry to families in Lee's Summit is making me feel a bit stagnant." I now realize much of this feeling stems from being impatient. I want to get this done. I want to run ahead, faster than the pace God wants me to go. As I pondered this I imagined myself as one of Jesus' 12 disciples. I saw myself running ahead saying, "Come on, Jesus! We're done here. Its time to move on." I imagine Jesus responding, "Slow down, Kevin. Don't run ahead of me. Be patient and listen. I have something for you here."

Pay Attention
An unfortunate by-product of impatience is missing the beautiful scenery along the way. The journey is just as important as the destination. Many of the lessons Jesus taught were learned on the journey to a destination (i.e. the woman at the well, road to Emmaus, etc). Too often I run ahead of Jesus. All the while, Jesus is walking at his 3 mile-an-hour pace wanting me to experience things along the way.

I am His Beloved
Countless times over my life I've heard it said, and proclaimed myself that Jesus loves me. I know this is true. I've experienced it. But being God's beloved isn't an occasional mountaintop experience used to keep me going until the next rush of love God pours over me. It is a constant state of existence. My humanity distracts me from this existence. I am flawed, constantly reminded of my need for God's grace and mercy. Over the past few weeks I've been reminded of how, as the songwriter says, *I am unaware these afflictions eclipsed by glory and I realize just how beautiful you are and how great your affections are for me.*

I met with Joe Wolters, executive director of soul care at Potter's Inn. He recommended I read *Life of the Beloved*, by Henri Nouwen. In the second chapter Nouwen writes, "Becoming the beloved means letting the truth of our belovedness become enfleshed in everything we think, say, or do. As long as 'being the beloved' is little more than a beautiful thought or a lofty idea that hangs above my life to keep me from becoming depressed, nothing really changes." Too often I've treated my belovedness as a boost to get me to the next plateau. My time at Potter's Inn highlighted my need to slow down, pay attention, and recognize God's love for me in every situation.

WORK HARD. PLAY HARD.

As I was contemplating this, God directed me to Jeremiah 9 and 10. These aren't the easiest chapters to read. Jeremiah is surrounded by idolatry. God's own people turned their back on His love. Jeremiah 9:23,24 says:

"This is what the Lord says:
Don't let the wise boast in their wisdom,
or the powerful boast in their power,
or the rich boast in their riches.
But those who wish to boast should boast in this alone,
that they truly know me and understand that I am the Lord who demonstrates unfailing love,
and who brings justice and righteousness to the earth,
and that I delight in these things.
I, the Lord, have spoken."

It was as if God sat right across from me, looked me in the eye and said, "Slow your pace. My love will never end, but you can run ahead of me and soon you will find yourself outside of my protection. And if you run too far you will forget what it's like to be my beloved."

Slow down, pay attention and enjoy the moment and live in my love for you.

Action steps:

1. Seek out and/or maintain providential relationships in 4 key areas (life coaching, spiritual direction, Biblical counseling, and Biblical discipleship).

2. Critique my schedule. Since taking on the role of Family pastor, I have dramatically increased the number of meetings I attend. Most of these are necessary. I anticipate more time needed to spend with parents and families this fall requiring me to constantly evaluate the purpose of every meeting making the most of my time. I also need to to a better job scheduling in time between meetings giving me opportunity to regain my focus and prepare for what is next.

3. Silence and solitude, both scheduled times and recognition when I need to step away from the noise. I need to tweak the way I approach my quiet time, mostly the place in which I go. I will find three or four better places to be alone and silent.

There are so many people who made this sabbatical possible. I want to thank the elders of LSCC. Not only did they encourage me, but established a policy for sabbaticals.

I want to thank the Family ministry team. Never once did I feel obligated to check my work email, make a phone call or even attend an LSCC service. I left for five weeks with complete confidence that the work of family ministry would be done.

The staff of LSCC has been very supportive and gracious to pick up my slack while I've been gone. I am blessed to be a part of this team.

Most importantly, I want to thank my wife Pam. She fully supported my time by being flexible giving me freedom to experience what God had planned for me.

What about you? Jesus moved at 3 miles-per-hour. How fast are you going?

Additional Resources

IMPORTANT NOTE: We aim to make readily available resources to you; however, this does not mean we endorse any of these sites or organizations, nor do we recommend that you use any of them. You can explore the references below—as well as those cited throughout this book, compiled in the Endnotes section—and tailor your sabbatical to your specific season of life and needs. Happy planning!

Practical Tools on Sabbaticals

Sabbatical Guide: https://app.rightnowmedia.org/en/content/details/795135

Soul Shepherding Institute - Soul Shepherding Institute Retreat (Remote access available)

Organizations to Look Into for Your Next Sabbatical

Billy's Home Place

The Oasis Beach House at
301 Jackson, Hollywood, FL 33019

The Lilly Endowment, Inc.

Ridgecrest Conference Center

Soul Shepherding Retreats

Focus on the Family: Pastor and Leader Retreat Centers

Stillwater Pastor Retreat

Articles You May Find Helpful

Research: THE TRANSFORMATIVE POWER OF SABBATICALS. Harvard Business Review. (2023b, February 23). https://hbr.org/2023/02/research-the-transformative-power-of-sabbaticals

Gaultiere, B. (2018, January 3). *A Sabbatical Guide For Pastors—Soul Shepherding.* Soul Shepherding - Following Jesus for Deeper Life and Greater Influence. https://www.soulshepherding.org/sabbatical-guide-pastors/#:~:text=A%20true%20Sabbatical%20is%20a%20season

Clifton, D. (2020, November 28). *Ministry sabbaticals: A pastor's guide.* Daily Pastor. https://dailypastor.com/ministry-sabbatical-guide-pastors/

How rest & sabbath can strengthen pastoral well-being. Barna Group. (2023, June 29). https://www.barna.com/research/rest-sabbath/

Clergy discounts. The Clergy Connection. (n.d.). https://theclergyconnection.blogspot.com/p/clergy-discounts.html

Retreats and vacation discounts for pastors' families. Hope For Pastors' Wives. (2022, May 19). https://

hopeforpastorswives.com/ministry-resources/retreat-locations/

Lastly, one article too good not to share on the role of the pastors and their day-to-day efforts: https://churchanswers.com/blog/fifteen-unusual-hospital-visits-experienced-by-pastors/

Other Books You May Want to Read

Planning Sabbaticals: A Guide for Congregations and their Pastors by Robert C. Saler

Sabbaticals: "how-to" take a break from ministry before ministry breaks you by Rusty McKie

A Sabbatical Primer for Churches: How to Love and Honor the Pastor God Has Given You by David C. Alves

Works Cited

Covey, S. R. (May 19, 2020). *The 7 Habits of Highly Effective People: 30th Anniversary Edition (The Covey Habits Series).* Simon & Schuster.

Hollis, W. C. (1962). *Sabbatical Leave in American Higher Education: Origin Early History and Current Practices.* U. S. Government Printing Office.

Hyatt, M. (2019). *Free to Focus—A total Productivity System to Achieve More by Doing Less.* Baker Books.

Alund, Natalie Neysa. "Texas Megachurch Pastor Matt Chandler Steps down after DMs with Woman 'Crossed a Line.'" USA TODAY. Accessed December 4, 2024. https://www.usatoday.com/story/news/nation/2022/08/30/megachurch-pastor-matt-chandler-instagram/7938054001/.

Billy's Home Place. "Billy's Home Place." Accessed December 2, 2024. https://www.billyshomeplace.org.

Blair, Leonardo, and Senior Reporter. "Megachurch Pastor Steps Away from Pulpit Because He Feels Far from God, Tired in Soul," December 11, 2019. https://www.christianpost.com/news/megachurch-pastor-steps-away-from-pulpit-because-he-feels-far-from-god-tired-in-soul.html.

Brumley, Jeff. "Yet Another Study Confirms: Many Pastors Are Hanging on by a Thread." Baptist News Global, April 28, 2022. https://baptistnews.com/article/yet-another-study-confirms-many-pastors-are-hanging-on-by-a-thread/.

BusinessAccelerator. "The Business Case for Sabbaticals." Accessed December 2, 2024. https://businessaccelerator.com/episodes/the-business-case-for-sabbaticals/.

Camera, ANTHONY HAHN | Boulder Daily. "Flatirons Community Church's Pastor Jim Burgen to Take Six-Month Sabbatical." *The Denver Post* (blog), June 12, 2019. https://www.denverpost.com/2019/06/11/flatirons-community-church-pastor-jim-burgen-sabbatical/.

Crosswalk.com. "Rob Bell Not the First Megachurch Pastor to Step Down." Accessed December 2, 2024. https://www.crosswalk.com/church/pastors-or-leadership/rob-bell-not-first-megachurch-pastor-to-step-down.html.

FranklinCovey. "Habit 7: Sharpen the Saw® | The 7 Habits of Highly Effective People®." Accessed December 2, 2024. https://www.franklincovey.com/the-7-habits/habit-7/.

"How a Physician Sabbatical Can Change Your Life." Accessed December 2, 2024. https://www.wolterskluwer.com/en/expert-insights/how-a-physician-sabbatical-can-change-your-life.

Hyatt, Michael. "I'm Going on a Sabbatical, and You Should Too." *Full Focus* (blog), July 31, 2017. https://fullfocus.co/why-sabbatical/.

"I'm Going on a Sabbatical, and You Should Too." *Full Focus* (blog), July 31, 2017. https://fullfocus.co/why-sabbatical/.

Ioppolo, Becky, and Steven Wooding. "How Academic Sabbaticals Are Used and How They Contribute to Research – a Small-Scale Study of the University of Cambridge Using Interviews and Analysis of Administrative Data." *F1000Research* 11 (March 14, 2023): 36. https://doi.org/10.12688/f1000research.74211.2.

Lea, Jessica. "WATCH: Pastor Explains How Elders Intervened Before a Burnout." *ChurchLeaders* (blog), June 12, 2019. https://churchleaders.com/pastors/videos-for-pastors/352525-flatirons-community-church-burnout.html.

WORKS CITED

Lilly Endowment. "Clergy Renewal Programs | Lilly Endowment Inc." Accessed December 2, 2024. https://lillyendowment.org/for-grantseekers/renewal-programs/pastors/.

McFall, Michael. "Council Post: A Strategic Sabbatical Can Help Your Employees Survive Burnout." Forbes. Accessed December 2, 2024. https://www.forbes.com/councils/forbesbusinesscouncil/2022/10/03/a-strategic-sabbatical-can-help-your-employees-survive-burnout/.

Morgan, Michael. "What I Learned About Sabbaticals by Finally Taking One." The Gospel Coalition, June 16, 2017. https://www.thegospelcoalition.org/article/what-i-learned-about-sabbaticals-by-finally-taking-one-2/.

"What I Learned About Sabbaticals by Finally Taking One." The Gospel Coalition, June 16, 2017. https://www.thegospelcoalition.org/article/what-i-learned-about-sabbaticals-by-finally-taking-one-2/.

Online Baptist Community. "The Perfect Pastor---Humor or Reality?," September 7, 2015. https://onlinebaptist.com/forums/topic/23894-the-perfect-pastor-humor-or-reality/.

"Pastoral Search Report | Bible.Org." Accessed December 2, 2024. https://bible.org/illustration/pastoral-search-report.

"Pastor-Ministry-Leader-Retreat-Centers.Pdf." Accessed December 2, 2024. https://www.focusonthefamily.com/wp-content/uploads/2020/09/Pastor-Ministry-Leader-Retreat-Centers.pdf.

Perry, Matthew R. "Why Are Preachers So Exhausted After Preaching?" *Bare Forests* (blog), June 26, 2020. https://drmattperry.com/2020/06/25/why-are-preachers-so-exhausted-after-preaching/.

Rachwani, Mostafa. "Hillsong Founder Brian Houston Steps down as Leader of Church." *The Guardian*, January 30, 2022, sec. World news.

https://www.theguardian.com/world/2022/jan/30/hillsong-founder-brian-houston-steps-down-as-leader-of-church.

Runkle, Larissa. "10 Unexpected Companies That Let You Take Sabbatical Leave." Text. The Penny Hoarder, June 27, 2023. World. https://www.thepennyhoarder.com/make-money/career/companies-offering-sabbaticals/.

"Sabbatarian Definition & Meaning - Merriam-Webster." Accessed December 2, 2024. https://www.merriam-webster.com/dictionary/Sabbatarian.

"Sabbatical | PayPal Benefits." Accessed December 2, 2024. https://www.paypalbenefits.com/us/emotional-wellness/sabbatical.

Time. "The Urgent Case for Sabbaticals for All," November 17, 2021. https://time.com/charter/6120287/sabbaticals-time-off-great-resignation/.

Time. "The Urgent Case for Sabbaticals for All," November 17, 2021. https://time.com/charter/6120287/sabbaticals-time-off-great-resignation/.

Endnotes

1. On medical field sabbaticals: "How a Physician Sabbatical Can Change Your Life," accessed December 2, 2024, https://www.wolterskluwer.com/en/expert-insights/how-a-physician-sabbatical-can-change-your-life.

2. On educational field sabbaticals: Becky Ioppolo and Steven Wooding, "How Academic Sabbaticals Are Used and How They Contribute to Research – a Small-Scale Study of the University of Cambridge Using Interviews and Analysis of Administrative Data," *F1000Research* 11 (March 14, 2023): 36, https://doi.org/10.12688/f1000research.74211.2.

3. Sample of a multinational sabbatical: "Sabbatical | PayPal Benefits," accessed December 2, 2024, https://www.paypalbenefits.com/us/emotional-wellness/sabbatical.

4. Peter Scazzero, *Emotionally Healthy Spirituality: It's Impossible to Be Spiritually Mature, While Remaining Emotionally Immature* (Zondervan, 2014).

5. Matthew R. Perry, "Why Are Preachers So Exhausted After Preaching?," *Bare Forests* (blog), June 26, 2020, https://drmattperry.com/2020/06/25/why-are-preachers-so-exhausted-after-preaching/.

6. Thank you Bible.org for this very credible story: "Pastoral Search Report | Bible.Org," accessed December 2, 2024, https://bible.org/illustration/pastoral-search-report.

7. Inspired by the article: "The Perfect Pastor---Humor or Reality?," Online Baptist Community, September 7, 2015, https://onlinebaptist.com/forums/topic/23894-the-perfect-pastor-humor-or-reality/.

8. "The Urgent Case for Sabbaticals for All," Time, November 17, 2021, https://time.com/charter/6120287/sabbaticals-time-off-great-resignation/.

9. Larissa Runkle, "10 Unexpected Companies That Let You Take Sabbatical Leave," Text, The Penny Hoarder, June 27, 2023, World,

https://www.thepennyhoarder.com/make-money/career/companies-offering-sabbaticals/.

10 Michael McFall, "Council Post: A Strategic Sabbatical Can Help Your Employees Survive Burnout," Forbes, accessed December 2, 2024, https://www.forbes.com/councils/forbesbusinesscouncil/2022/10/03/a-strategic-sabbatical-can-help-your-employees-survive-burnout.

11 "The Business Case for Sabbaticals," BusinessAccelerator, accessed December 2, 2024, https://businessaccelerator.com/episodes/the-business-case-for-sabbaticals/.

12 You can learn more about it here: "Habit 7: Sharpen the Saw® | The 7 Habits of Highly Effective People®," FranklinCovey, accessed December 2, 2024, https://www.franklincovey.com/the-7-habits/habit-7/.

13 "The Urgent Case for Sabbaticals for All," Time, November 17, 2021, https://time.com/charter/6120287/sabbaticals-time-off-great-resignation/.

14 Michael Hyatt, "I'm Going on a Sabbatical, and You Should Too," *Full Focus* (blog), July 31, 2017, https://fullfocus.co/why-sabbatical/.

15 Hyatt; Michael Hyatt, "I'm Going on a Sabbatical, and You Should Too," *Full Focu*s (blog), July 31, 2017, https://fullfocus.co/why-sabbatical/.

16 Follow this citation for more details: Michael Morgan, "What I Learned About Sabbaticals by Finally Taking One," The Gospel Coalition, June 16, 2017, https://www.thegospelcoalition.org/article/what-i-learned-about-sabbaticals-by-finally-taking-one-2/.

17 Leonardo Blair and Senior Reporter, "Megachurch Pastor Steps Away from Pulpit Because He Feels Far from God, Tired in Soul," December 11, 2019, https://www.christianpost.com/news/megachurch-pastor-steps-away-from-pulpit-because-he-feels-far-from-god-tired-in-soul.html.

18 ANTHONY HAHN | Boulder Daily Camera, "Flatirons Community Church's Pastor Jim Burgen to Take Six-Month Sabbatical," *The Denver*

Post (blog), June 12, 2019, https://www.denverpost.com/2019/06/11/flatirons-community-church-pastor-jim-burgen-sabbatical/.

19 Natalie Neysa Alund, "Texas Megachurch Pastor Matt Chandler Steps down after DMs with Woman 'Crossed a Line,'" USA TODAY, accessed December 4, 2024, https://www.usatoday.com/story/news/nation/2022/08/30/megachurch-pastor-matt-chandler-instagram/7938054001/.

20 Jeff Brumley, "Yet Another Study Confirms: Many Pastors Are Hanging on by a Thread," Baptist News Global, April 28, 2022, https://baptistnews.com/article/yet-another-study-confirms-many-pastors-are-hanging-on-by-a-thread/.

21 Mostafa Rachwani, "Hillsong Founder Brian Houston Steps down as Leader of Church," T*he Guardian*, January 30, 2022, sec. World news, https://www.theguardian.com/world/2022/jan/30/hillsong-founder-brian-houston-steps-down-as-leader-of-church.

22 "Rob Bell Not the First Megachurch Pastor to Step Down," Crosswalk.com, accessed December 2, 2024, https://www.crosswalk.com/church/pastors-or-leadership/rob-bell-not-first-megachurch-pastor-to-step-down.html.

23 Michael Morgan, "What I Learned About Sabbaticals by Finally Taking One," The Gospel Coalition, June 16, 2017, https://www.thegospelcoalition.org/article/what-i-learned-about-sabbaticals-by-finally-taking-one-2/.

24 Referring to the late 1590s naval tradition for ships to lower their flags when in the presence of the Pope or the king of Spain as a sign of deference and respect. In this context, to "not dip your colors" means to never yield to any person, country, or authority other than Christ.

25 Jessica Lea, "WATCH: Pastor Explains How Elders Intervened Before a Burnout," *ChurchLeaders* (blog), June 12, 2019, https://churchleaders.com/pastors/videos-for-pastors/352525-flatirons-community-church-burnout.html.

26 "Sabbatarian Definition & Meaning - Merriam-Webster," accessed December 2, 2024, https://www.merriam-webster.com/dictionary/Sabbatarian.

27 "Clergy Renewal Programs | Lilly Endowment Inc.," Lilly Endowment, accessed December 2, 2024, https://lillyendowment.org/for-grantseekers/renewal-programs/pastors/.

28 "Pastor-Ministry-Leader-Retreat-Centers.Pdf," accessed December 2, 2024, https://www.focusonthefamily.com/wp-content/uploads/2020/09/Pastor-Ministry-Leader-Retreat-Centers.pdf.

29 www.vrbo.com and enter 301 Jackson, Hollywood, FL 33019 or visit our Facebook page to find more about the Oasis Beach House at https://www.facebook.com/profile.php?id=100063570942598

30 "Billy's Home Place," Billy's Home Place, accessed December 2, 2024, https://www.billyshomeplace.org.

www.ingramcontent.com/pod-product-compliance
Lightning Source LLC
Chambersburg PA
CBHW051948290426
44110CB00015B/2156